After Paradise

Also by Jon Thompson:

Poetry
The Book of the Floating World

Criticism
Fiction, Crime, and Empire: Clues to Modernity and Postmodernism

Jon Thompson

After Paradise

Essays on the Fate of American Writing

Shearsman Books
Exeter

Published in the United Kingdom in 2009 by
Shearsman Books Ltd
58 Velwell Road
Exeter EX4 4LD

ISBN 978-1-84861-041-5
First Edition

Acknowledgements

It gives me great pleasure to thank Thomas Lisk, John Kessel, John David
Smith and Richard Marshall for their support for this book. For generous
readings and suggestions, I'm indebted to Nick Halpern, Keith Tuma, Patrick
McGee, Tony Lopez, Daniel Tiffany and Susan Howe. I owe a special debt of
gratitude to Declan Kiberd and Tony Harrison who gave continuous support
for this, most unlikely, project. And lastly, to Tony Frazer, who actually turned
it into a book—many thanks.

My gratitude, also, to the editors of the following journals who first published
essays from *After Paradise*: *The Massachusetts Review, Fascicle, Kiosk* and
Identity Theory.

CONTENTS

To Zoë and Sofie—readers of the future

What a noise the words make
writing themselves.
  —Michael Palmer, 'Construction of the Museum'

Speak and say the immaculate syllables
That he spoke only by doing what he did.

God and angels, this was his desire,
Whose head lies blurring here, for this he died.
  —Wallace Stevens, 'The Men That are Falling'

Always the same. The deliberate consciousness of Americans so
fair and smooth-spoken, and the under-consciousness so devilish.
Destroy! destroy! destroy! hums the underconsciouness. *Love and
produce! Love and produce!* Cackles the upper consciousness. And
the world hears only the Love-and-produce cackle. Refuses to
hear the hum of destruction underneath. Until such time as we
will *have* to hear.
  —D.H. Lawrence,
    Studies in Classic American Literature

There is hurt within the word.
Word that hurts and, strangely, comforts.
Mystery of its strangeness.
  —Edmond Jabès, *A Foreigner Carrying in the
    Crook of His Arm a Tiny Book*

Chapter 1
William Bradford's *Of Plymouth Plantation*:
Puritan Cannibalism in the New World

"Thus out of small beginnings . . ."
—William Bradford

(The lost book of a lost people, wandering, too, through history, wandering in and out of this moment, a moment which never stays *put*. The book surfaces from a distant past, a past of arcane religious feuds and schisms, a time of zealotry and persecutions. The temptation: to lapse into history-as-chronology, the divide of centuries, and end by denying the inheritance because it *cannot be seen*, traced in a standard lineage—which only testifies to the tyranny of the seen. And yet signs of it are unmistakable: without it, I would not be where I am, who I am, like so many others, descendent, son, inheritor, scratching out a history and a future not of my own making . . .)

Bradford's book anticipated this one, made the space for it, *made* it . . .

Of Plymouth Plantation: a new Book of Revelations in which the Word of God makes itself manifest in a wilderness of hieroglyphs. Bradford's God is alive in the language of his book, which draws on the Bible, but longs to become the book of books, the text of the world that will envelop all others, supplant all others—even this one. The Word has an aural power, an aural authority: to define the past and the future . . .

Sanctification of the Word: rather than seeing language as a threat to the dissemination of the Word (diffusion), the Puritans sanctified language itself. (Or, perhaps, *because* of its power of diffusion, it was sanctified). If language could be transubstantiated, moved from naming to invocation, then speaking and writing—all signification—could be a way of honoring God, a form of fealty to divine authority, a kind of prayer. Hence the prestige of writing in Puritan culture . . .

Yet language, too, is distrusted. Puritan writing longs for the unitary wholeness of a pre-linguistic state, to apprehend God directly rather than through the veil of language. Language is consecrated in part because it is an unavoidable expedient, but it is also distrusted as a second-order means of signification. This accounts for the Puritan reverence for silence: signification without signification . . .

The Word itself is performative, active, dynamic: it damns and redeems. It does not so much reflect the world as is; it is an emissary of the world to come. As a particle of God, it is invested with the divine power of change. By internalizing the Word of God, the Pilgrims help to bring about the world to come. The Word as Janus-faced: one face looks backward in time to the Word-made-flesh in the Scriptures; one is future-oriented, looks toward a future that resembles an imagined past: a New Jerusalem. Traveling toward the future is also a return to the past—a past that never was . . .

Persecution as a sign of God's election: for the Pilgrims, as for the first Christians, persecution proved their righteousness, and the world's corrupted state. Suffering is redemptive inasmuch as it is a means of bringing the elect into a visionary state of being. Indeed, God authors suffering so that his elect will come to understand his Word. Suffering, even martyrdom, educates them into an understanding of divine purpose; it becomes a *necessary* prerequisite for seeing it: "[. . .] they bore sundry years with much patience, till they were occasioned by the continuance and increase of these troubles, and other means which the Lord raised up in those days, to see further into things by the light of the Word of God."

Transparency of the soul: the greatest desire of the Pilgrims—and their greatest fear.

For them, the world has no autonomy, no being-in-itself, being-for-itself; it exists only as a means of fulfilling the promise of a New Jerusalem. Puritan arrogance: the world exists only for *us*, to teach *us*, to redeem *us*. (That arrogance, our ancestral curse . . .)

Bradford's Book of Revelations is written to future generations as a testament of faith; through this witness, future generations will know how to preserve God's work. The Book of Revelations of the New Israelites will be the Book of the Future, the book of all futures. Yet writing, for Bradford the historian, is an effort bent upon *arresting* futurity. By relegating time and change to an unchanging narrative in which submission to the Word is exalted as redemption, the martyrdom of the particular is offered as the means of deliverance.

The Puritan imagination of the New World: in their mind's eye, the Puritans saw it as a vast, unpeopled land. The work of that imagination would be to bring reality into compliance with itself, that image of a nation. That imagination acknowledged the existence of native peoples, but they were not seen as people, but as "wild beasts," to be dealt with as such. "The place they had thoughts on was some of those vast and unpeopled countries of America, which are fruitful and fit for habitation, being devoid of all civil inhabitants, where there are only savage and brutish men which range up and down, little otherwise than the wild beasts of the same." This invitation to extermination is intrinsic to the design of this Book of Revelations. Absolutism demands the abolition of all unsettling difference, and so it is that the dream of a New Jerusalem can be founded without shame upon genocide dreams, spiritual regeneration upon violence . . .

Whence this righteousness? From God's Word, which for the Puritans, speaks the language of absolutes. To be godly, therefore, is also to speak a language of absolutes, to avoid trafficking in the fallen, debased languages of qualification—which is not now an idiolect . . .

In a world divided into Good and Evil, Good will always partake of Evil . . .

"And I may not omit here a special work of God's providence. There was a proud and very profane young man, one of the sea man, of a lusty, able body, which made him the more haughty; he would always be condemning the poor people in their sickness and cursing them daily with grievous execrations; and did not let to tell them that he hoped to help to cast half of them overboard before they came to their journey's end, and to make merry with what they had; and if he were by any gently reproved, he would curse and swear most bitterly. But it pleased God before they came half seas over, to smite this young man with a grievous disease, of which he died in a desperate manner, and so was himself the first that was thrown overboard." To Bradford the sin of pride in relation to Puritanism itself is not a possibility.

Puritan cannibalism: having fled Holland—in part due to a fear of assimilation—Bradford projects a similar fear onto the indigenous peoples of North America, who are presented as not only mindlessly violent sadists, but as cannibalistic connoisseurs, who long to take in, *assimilate*—the flesh of the Puritans. In his journal, Bradford's imagination lingers over the image of a dismembered body, a blasphemous version of communion: "And also those who should escape or overcome these difficulties should yet be in continual danger of the savage people, who are cruel, barbarous, most treacherous, being most furious in their rage and merciless where they overcome; not being only content to kill and take away life, but delight to torment men in the most bloody manner that may be; flaying some alive with the shells of fishes, cutting off the members and joints of others by piecemeal and broiling on the coals, eat the collops of their flesh in their sight whilst they live, with other cruelties horrible to relate." What is being cannibalized here is not only flesh, but the Word-made-flesh: the godliness of the Puritans is lost within pagan bodies. The fear here is the fear not merely of physical violation, but the fear of a loss of identity within the "wilderness" of the New World.

This *imagined* cannibalism describes an attitude of revulsion— and fascination. Indeed, the fate of the dismembered body is *desired*: as a metonym for Christ's tortured body, the violence visited upon it is a sign of God's election. To be dismembered is to be sacrificed, but it is also to be made spiritually whole . . .

The body in pain: testament to a faith beyond words (in Bradford's imagination, the consumed bodies are *voiceless*, their silence symbolizes a ecstatic union with Christ through a New World Calvary). It is this voicelessness that Bradford longs to speak for, needs to speak for, speaks *for* . . .

Of Plymouth Plantation yearns, implicitly, for Christ-like mutilation: in the body's resemblance to Christ's crucified body lives the hope of resurrection, of becoming one with God.

In Bradford's text, the body appears dramatically in a prostrate state—ill bodies, dying bodies, wounded bodies, suffering bodies, dead bodies. The afflicted body is the only body worthy of representation. The healthy body offers no lessons, teaches nothing, unless it is the lesson of the exception. The healthy body: invisible. The afflicted body: a sign of God's love—or punishment; at any rate, a sign *of* God . . .

Anno Domini 1634: "This spring also, those Indians that lived about their trading houses there, fell sick of the small pox and died most miserably; for a sorer disease cannot befall them, they fear it more than the plague. For usually they that have this disease have them in abundance, and for want of bedding and linen and other helps they fall into a lamentable condition as they lie on their hard mats, the pox breaking and mattering and running one into another, their skin cleaving by reason thereof to the mats they lie on. When they turn them a whole side will flay at once as it were and they will be all of a gore blood, most fearful to behold. And then being very sore, what with cold and other distempers, they die like rotten sheep. The condition of this people was so lamentable and they fell down so generally of this disease as they were in the end not able to help one another, no not to make a fire, nor to fetch a little water to drink, nor any bury the dead. But would strive as long as they could, and when they could procure no other means to make fire, they would burn the wooden trays and dishes they ate their meat in, and their very bows and arrows. And some would crawl out on all fours to get a little water, and sometimes die by the way and not be able to get in again [. . .] But by the marvelous goodness and providence of God, not one of the English was so much as sick or in the least measure tainted with this disease, though they daily did these offices for them many weeks together." This is illness as punishment for paganism; their illness confirms the Puritans in their goodness (a different goodness from the goodness which, in their extremity, the English showed to them).

Purtian humility: Anno Domini 1637: [The Pequot War] The assault on the Pequot: "So they went on, and so ordered their march as the Indians [i.e. the Narragansett, who allied themselves with the English]brought them to a fort of the enemy's (in which most of their chief men were) before day. They approached the same with great silence and surrounded it both with English and Indians, that they might not break out; and so assaulted them [the Pequot] with great courage, shooting amongst them, and entered the fort with all speed. And those that first entered, found sharp resistance from the enemy who both shot at and grappled with them; others ran into their houses and brought out fire and set them on fire, which soon took in their mat; and standing close together, with the wind all was quickly on a flame, and thereby more were burnt to death than was otherwise slain. It burnt their bowstrings and made them unserviceable; those that scaped the fire were slain with the sword, some hewed to pieces, others run through with their rapiers, so as they were quickly dispatched and very few escaped. It was conceived they thus destroyed about 400 at this time. It was a fearful sight to see them thus frying in the fire and the streams of blood quenching the same, and horrible was the stink and scent thereof; but the victory seemed a sweet sacrifice, and they gave the praise thereof to God, who had wrought so wonderfully for them, thus to enclose their enemies in their hands and give them so speedy a victory over so proud and insulting an enemy." Oh the *force* of humility, which makes the "sweet sacrifice" an offering, a blood-prayer, to God . . .

Puritan time: an always-increasing measurement of the temporal separation from Calvary until the present moment and the always-decreasing amount of time that separates one from a (longed-for) union with Christ in the afterlife. Puritan time is thus the domain of exquisite anticipation and suffering: a trembling of fear and desire. To be Puritan is to have an intense awareness of one's *inbetweeness*, an awareness of distance from God and (a hoped-for) union with Him, an awareness that reveals itself in the anxious notation of the texture of everyday life: *here is the life I've lived, here is my record of accomplishment.*

For the Pilgrims, the New World represents the possibility of freedom, but also, necessarily, unfreedom, a challenge to the integrity of the self, a testing ground, a site for the destruction of the self—a New Calvary as much as a New Jerusalem . . .

Despite their superficial abhorrence of the pagan, the Puritans of Plymouth are irresistibly drawn to it, for the pagan confirms the existence of the godly; because they are ungodly, the Puritans can be godly. Their savagery, brutality, and irrationality confirms the Puritans in their belief of their own religiosity, civilization and mercy. No wonder Bradford is fascinated by them: their utter difference assures him of his own virtue. They assuage the anxiety deep in the soul of any religious schismatic: am I right? Hence the Puritan ambivalence vis-à-vis Native Americans: they feared them, but were obsessed by them; their sheer difference compelled the Puritans to bring their other-worldliness into the orbit of their own belief system in order to validate it as singular. In the end, it is the Puritans who desire— *need*—to cannibalize the natives, not vice-versa . . .

In the historiography of the Pilgrims, there is no difference between an imagined reality and actuality: the scene of cannibalism is imagined, but it is presented as fact. Stone-cold pragmatists, the Puritans were also great inventors of the real. The writing of history: not merely a way of re-envisioning the world but a means of re-inventing it . . .

The face of savagery: "It is recorded in Scripture as a mercy to the Apostle and his shipwrecked company, that the barbarians showed them no small kindness in refreshing them, but these savage barbarians, when they met with them (as after will appear) were readier to fill their sides with arrows than otherwise. And for the seasons it was winter, and they that know the winters of that country know them to be sharp and violent and subject to cruel and fierce storms, dangerous to travel to known places, much more to search an unknown coast. Besides, what could they see but a hideous and desolate wilderness, full of wild beasts and wild men—and what multitudes there might be of them they knew not. Neither could they, as it were, go up to the top of Pisgah to view from this wilderness a more goodly country to feed their hopes; for which way soever they turned their eyes (saved upward to the heavens) they could have little solace or content in respect of outward objects. For summer being done, all things stand upon them with a weatherbeaten face, and the whole country, full of woods and thickets, represented a wild and savage hue." Savagery incarnate in the very landscape of the New World: the savagery of the inhabitants is mirrored by the savagery of the land. To the Puritans, the very land had the face of savagery. This is a savagery that *demands* to be subdued, a savagery which calls out to the Puritans for relief . . .

(Unsaid: the fate of Dorothy Bradford, Bradford's first wife, who after gazing at the desolate sand dunes of Cape Cod for weeks, threw herself into Cape Cod harbor in despair: the first Puritan victim of the Puritan view of the land).

That savagery not only confirmed the Pilgrims in their sense of the superiority of their theocracy, but it also meant that *they* could not be savage, since the New World, and its inhabitants, were thought to possess a monopoly on it. Because they, as a community, were God's elect, they could not, *as a community*, do evil. In the New World, the history of evil is of a foreign agent which must be exiled, cast out, exorcised so that the polity can return to a state of unstained goodness. This is a reflex of all theocracies, but in the New World, the reflex remains alive long after the theocracy has expired.

The Word speaks a messianic language of imperatives: there is no other Right than this Right, no other Good than this one. Otherness is divinity negated—evil. (This a voice from the past, from childhood, spoken from love, spoken with love; rejected, it nevertheless clings to me . . .).

In rendering his community in the third person plural rather than the first person plural, Bradford explicitly transforms the travails of the Separatists of Plymouth into myth, a re-enactment of Biblical tribulation in which the they play the role of the persecuted Jews. Through the distance achieved by this pronoun usage, he can be seen to be transforming himself and others into characters in a theological drama. The writing of history is not only the record of God's intervention on behalf of his people, but it is also a prayer to God for succor. Call and response, call and response: Puritan writing aspires to abolish the status of writing as a separate system of signs for the world, words standing in for things, in order to remake it as one with the world, not separate, not different, but a sign system, mystically whole, in which invested with God's presence, the word communes with the world . . .

The narrator of *Of Plymouth Plantation*: a ghost that haunts the establishment of Plymouth Plantation. But a ghost that cannot allow itself to acknowledge its own spectral nature . . .

If symbols can be abolished, everything can be a signature of God's presence . . .

A future text: *Of Plymouth Plantation* is written from the point of view of the future: Bradford's point of view floats above and beyond the immediate present to narrate events from the perspective of the future, which surveys contemporary achievements as those of a now-distant past: "What could now sustain them but the Spirit of God and His grace? May not and ought not the children of these fathers rightly say "Our fathers were Englishmen, which came over this great ocean, and were ready to perish in this wilderness; but they cried unto the Lord, and He heard their voice, and looked on their great adversity," etch [sic].' This point of view confers upon the Puritans an heroic aura, but against the failures of Plymouth Plantation, it also establishes the hope that future generations will redeem the covenant, whatever its state of disarray *at the time of writing* . . .

Of Plymouth Plantation—is a narrative of deliverance—deliverance from English persecution and religious corruption, deliverance from the seductions of Dutch culture, deliverance from the high seas, deliverance from Indians, deliverance from the harshness of a New England winter, deliverance from illness, deliverance from the ungodly who accompanied the Puritans to the New World, deliverance from treachery, deliverance from conspiracy and intrigue. God is both the author of this suffering and their means of deliverance. Yet even God cannot deliver them from themselves. The New Jerusalem cannot be made by God; in theory, it can only be made by man. And by what he writes and imagines as much as by what he *does* . . .

Of Plymouth Plantation: a book of letters, letters to friends, supporters in England, letters of succor, faith, testament; letters of trade, financial woes, material desperation, prosperity; letters of appeal; letters to God, to future generations and past ones; letters received of every kind. All *dispatches*, intent upon closing the divide between here and there, past and present, present and future, the world that is and the world that is imagined . . .

God as author: the vexing of responsibility. That is the *curse* of the blessing . . .

In the Mayflower Compact (1620), the agreement to a common set of laws for all is not simply done on behalf of the signatories involved; it is done "for the Glory of God and advancement of the Christian Faith and Honor of our King and Country." The compact only has meaning inasmuch as it serves as a means of advancing Christendom and England's interests in the New World. Without these larger legitimizing presences, the political achievement of the Compact would be nugatory. In the New World, there has always been the felt need for a transcendental validation for the actions of Europeans; only God can sanction the unsanctionable . . .

God *of* language. The Mayflower Compact begins by invoking God: "In the name of God, Amen." God is not unnameable, unsignifiable; quite the opposite. The assurance that the world is "just so" starts with the assurance that God is identifiable, known, nameable. This is radically different from the unsignifiable YAHWEH of the ancient Hebrews; the unnameable dimension of God's existence signified the radical otherness of God, his existence outside human systems of representation. God's otherness made them elect—but it also demanded that they be outsiders, exiles in the world. While the Puritans also were exiles, God's elect, their sense of exile was softened by the assurance of a God with whom they could have intercourse. By naming Him, they fostered the hope of familiarity.

The invocation to God exists to bless the accord, but it also exists to embody God's presence in language so that language will be a vessel for God's will, so that it will not be other, so that the Word can be made flesh. This is the *hope* of the invocation.

What is sworn to in the Mayflower Compact is a "Civil Body Politic, for our better ordering and preservation and furtherance of the ends aforesaid; and by virtue hereof to enact, constitute, and frame such just and equal Laws, Ordinances, Acts, Constitutions and Offices, from time to time, as shall be thought most meet and convenient for the general good of the Colony, unto which we promise all due submission and obedience." Submission: a posture the Puritans knew in their very bones. The Law could become a new God. A civil body politic—but one that is now deified, worshipped and observed with the faithfulness of a zealot. As well as the non-observances, the blindness, that every zealot permits himself . . .

A rhetoric of God: Over and over, Bradford employs a particular rhetoric to describe God's interventions on behalf of the Pilgrims, viz. "it pleased God . . ." as in "Thus it pleased God to vanquish their enemies and give them deliverance; and by His special providence so to dispose that not any one of them were either hurt or hit" or, "The spring now approaching, it pleased God the mortality began to cease among them, and the sick and the lame recovered apace, which put as [it] were new life into them, though they had borne their sad affliction with much patience and contentedness as I think any people could do." A God that can be pleased is a God that can be displeased; Bradford's rhetoric depicts a God of mysterious and mercurial temperament: a God who creates hardship so as to grant mercy. A God who sacrifices *and* relents, a God who jealously demands obeisance *and* constant attention. A God who needs the Puritans as much as they need Him . . .

The Starving Time: A time to die *into* the New World—and to be reborn.

The gravest sin, the greatest taboo in Puritan culture: disappointment in God. It is that which cannot be permitted, the unthinkable—Bradford's text is endlessly inventive in the ways in which it refuses disappointment, remains determinedly secure in his faith. Herein lay the seeds of American optimism, which likewise, makes disappointment in God (the ideal, the nation, the future) a taboo . . .

Lords of Misrule: "And Morton became Lord of Misrule, and maintained (as it were) a School of Atheism. And after they had got some goods into their hands, and got much by trading with the Indians, they spent it as vainly in quaffing and drinking, both wine and strong waters in great excess (and, as some reported) £10 worth in the morning. They also set up a maypole, drinking and dancing about it many days together, inviting the Indian women for their consorts, dancing and frisking together like so many fairies or furies, rather; and worse practices. As if they had anew revived and celebrated the feasts of the Roman goddess Flora, or the beastly practices of the mad Bacchanalians. Morton likewise, to show his poetry composed sundry rhymes and verses, some tending to lasciviousness, and others to the detraction and scandal of some persons, which he affixed to this idle or idol maypole. They changed also the name of their place, and instead of calling it Mount Wollaston they called it Merry-mount, as if this jollity would have lasted ever." Having established a "rule," the Puritans could not accept any order antagonistic to it, especially one bent upon satirizing them: parody is impermissible in Paradise. How swiftly the dispossessors take on the robes of justice! How swiftly theft becomes "rule"!

(Provoked repeatedly by Morton, the Pilgrims had his house burned down; another "rule" behind the visible one . . .)

Disorder is often cast as misrule, but the most serious forms of misrule are invariably the most upright, the most *orderly* . . .

A rhetoric of the fantastic: one of Bradford's favorite qualifications is the paradoxical phrase "as it were." In describing Morton's selling of rifles to the Algonquin, for example, he writes: "So as when they saw the execution that a piece would do, and the benefit that might come by the same, they became mad (as it were) after them and would not stick to give any price they could attain to for them: accounting their bows and arrows but baubles in comparison of them." "As it were" allows for the assertion of the fantastic along with the qualification of it. Through "as it were" the extraordinary becomes ordinary, believable. In *Of Plymouth Plantation* it possesses a magical authority inasmuch as it permits the location of the extraordinary in the ordinary, the supernatural within the natural: "The spring now approaching, it pleased God the mortality began to cease among them, and the sick and the lame recovered apace, which put as [it] were new life into them, though they had borne their sad affliction with much patience and contentedness as I think any people could do." "As it were" blurs the lines between the extraordinary and the ordinary. It asserts that language is a figure of speech and a straightforward accounting of the way things are (or were). The radical deep logic of "as it were," which ultimately holds that all of reality is nothing but language, figures of speech, is held in check by a God who is one with the word and one with the world.

Yet "as it were" cannot help but testify, as it were, to the presence *and* absence of God.

The Puritan teleology of redemption makes the world "as it were."

Madness for exchange, madness in exchange: the first and most lasting of diseases brought over from the Old World. An economy of exchange will erase the world that was and usher in an endless series of new ones (the doom of Plymouth Plantation).

Madness: *illegitimate exchanges.*

Writing too: a desire to exchange one reality for another, a wish to replace one reality for another.

Indians in Heaven? Buried in a section entitled "A Voyage in Search of Corn," is the following passage: "So they put into Manamoyick Bay and got with [what] they could there. In this place Squanto fell sick of an Indian fever, bleeding much at the nose (which the Indians take for a symptom of death) and within a few days died there; desiring the Governor to pray for him that he might go to the Englishman's God in Heaven; and bequeathed sundry of his things to sundry of his English friends as remembrances of his love; of whom they had a great loss." To admit him, to relent, God would have to relinquish his Kingdom . . .

How right of Squanto! It was indeed the *Englishman's* God he came to know: a God made in their own image. The translator of the English to the Indians wants, in the end, to be translated into *Englishness*, a minor idol. And the poignancy of his innocence: as if the English had only *one* God . . .

The proof of the invisible is the visible; indeed, the invisible requires the realm of the visible in order to manifest itself. The visible world as palimpsest: pressed into the service of rendering evidence of the invisible, it cannot be for itself; within the Puritan worldview, it has to *betoken* something else.

Nature: the signs—or hieroglyphs—of God. Puritan prayer—one signifying system beseeching God for signs it can translate back into itself: signs taken for wonders. *All* change is Providential; by contrast, lack of change is tainted with divine disfavor, or most unsettling, the absence of God. Lack of change perturbs the Puritan obsession with interpretation, the need to find God in the wilderness, the need to discover His plan. If everything appears the same, day after day, week after week, God is not signifying himself; the anxiety, unspoken, but desperate, is the fear that God is gone, and his elect has been abandoned in a world that can never be remade: "By a great drought which continued from the third week in May, till about the middle of July, without any rain and with great heat for the most part, insomuch as the corn began to wither away though it was set with fish, the moisture whereof helped it much. Yet at length it began to languish sore, and some of the drier grounds were parched like withered hay, part whereof was never recovered. Upon which they set a solemn day of humiliation, to seek the Lord by humble and fervent prayer, in this great distress. And He was pleased to give them a gracious and speedy answer, both to their own and the Indians' great admiration that lived amongst them. For all the morning, and the greatest part of the day, it was clear weather and very hot, and not a cloud or any sign of rain to be seen; yet toward evening it began to overcast, and shortly after to rain with such sweet and gentle showers as gave them cause of rejoicing and blessing God. It came without either wind or thunder or any violence, and by degrees, in that abundance that the earth was thoroughly wet and soaked and therewith. Which did so apparently revive and quicken the decayed corn and other fruits as was wonderful to see, and made the Indians astonished to behold."

Much of *Of Plymouth Plantation* is the record of the financial accountants of Plymouth—pounds and percentages. The fetishization of accounts is itself a form of godliness. The minute record of mundane expenses is not mundane, however: it is a record of the costs of building a New Jerusalem in the New World. Here finances and godliness are not antagonistic: the former is a means of achieving the latter. Thriftiness and careful husbandry of financial resources represents faithfulness to God's plan. Financial success is not only a form of virtue; it is a form of prayer.

The longing to be completely *transparent* in behavior and motivation is the chief longing underwriting *Of Plymouth Plantation*. Transparency before God, before the bar of public opinion, before the judgment of future generations: candor issues from his writing as a sign of virtue. And yet Bradford's history strains at its self-appointed task; it is fissured by the impossibility of the ambition, as when he sums up the falling out the Pilgrims had with Roger Williams: "Mr. Roger Williams, a man godly and zealous, having many precious parts but very unsettled in judgment, came over first to Massachusetts; but upon some discontent left that place and came hither, where he was friendly entertained according to their poor ability, and exercised his gifts amongst them and after some time was admitted a member of the church. And his teaching well approved, for the benefit whereof I still bless God, and am thankful to him even for his sharper admonitions and reproofs so far as they agreed with truth. He this year began to fall into some strange opinions to practice, which caused some controversy between the church and him. And in the end some discontent on his part, by occasion whereof he left them something abruptly. Yet afterwards sued for his dismission to the church of Salem, which was granted, with some caution to them concerning him and what care they ought to have of him. But he soon fell into more things there, both to their and the government's trouble and disturbance. I shall not need to name particulars; they are too well known now to all, though for a time the church here went under some hard censure by his occasion from some that afterwards smarted themselves. But he is to be pitied and prayed for; and so I shall leave the matter and desire the Lord to show him his errors and reduce him into the way of truth and give him a settled judgment and constancy in the same, for I hope he belongs to the Lord, and that He will show him mercy." The reasons for Williams's dissent are deliberately obscured; rather than transparency, there is opacity—and the suggestion is that Williams is a talented but misguided individual, a compulsive trouble-maker, a malcontent, who is wanting in the virtues of restraint and good judgment. Pity: the rhetorical means by which the self-deceived are banished, and the righteous claim their ascendancy. To be in the company of a lofty pity is to be in the presence of an unbearable arrogance—and an equally insupportable ignorance.

(Unsaid: One of Williams's "strange opinions" that occasioned disagreement with the Puritans at Plymouth was his insistence that the king's patent was invalid and only a direct purchase from the Indians would yield a just title to the land.)

Pity: the gesture that refuses transparency, that hides—enfolds—something unsayable.

American pity for other: bottomless . . .

The Law in Paradise must be at least as harsh as the Law in the Old World. Death-as-punishment is needed as much here as it was in the Old World—perhaps more, since the stakes are higher (a theocracy cannot afford the contagion of even venial sin). Death becomes in Paradise the right hand of righteousness: "This year [1630] John Billington the elder, one that came over with the first, was arraigned, and both by grand and petty jury found guilty of wilful murder, by plain and notorious evidence. And was for the same accordingly executed. This, as it was the first execution amongst them, so it was as a matter of great sadness unto them. They used all due means about his trial and took the advice of Mr. Winthrop and other the ablest gentlemen in Bay of the Massachusetts, that were then newly come over, who concurred with them that he ought to die, and the land to be purged from his blood. He and some of his had been often punished for miscarriages before, being one of the profanest families among them; they came from London, and I know not by what friends shuffled into their company. His fact was that he waylaid a young man, one John Newcomen, about a former quarrel and shot him with a gun, whereof he died."

The land purged from his blood: the Puritan fear of contagion, moral contagion, requires a cleansing of blood from the land, a cleansing that, paradoxically, requires the shedding of blood. (How much blood there was in Plymouth Plantation!) The insistence upon the land as morally blighted by human action can only happen when it is regarded as holy. And once compromised, that holiness demands a commensurate sacrifice to re-establish its purity.

Puritan double-vision: having turned its back upon the world, the Puritan community in the New World becomes hyper-aware of "the eyes of the world." To truly succeed, it must see respect in the eyes of the world it abandoned . . .

The dramatic Puritan self: an anarchic thing, corrupt and corrupting, a grotesque bundle of unbridled passions subdued only by God's power and grace (cf. Edward Taylor: "Unclean, Unclean: My Lord, Undone, all Vile,/Yea, all Defiled: What shall Thy servant do?/Unfit for Thee: not fit for Holy Soil,/Nor for communion of Saints below./A bag of botches, Lump of Loathsomeness:/Defiled by Touch, by Issue: Leproused flesh."). A thing to suspect, to destroy—because it too contains yearnings, desires, impulses, imperatives which are *other* (alien to "goodness"). Hostile to the world without and to the world within, Puritanism always expressed itself—in terms of love and hate—in a rhetoric of *discipline*. *"Because I love you, I discipline you; because I hate you, I discipline you."* The Puritan will-to-discipline involves the implicit recognition that the internal and external worlds are ungovernable, uncontrollable. Discipline provides the fiction of control—and when that control breaks down, dramatically implodes, discipline is invoked as the *solution.* As a mode of human interaction, discipline ensures that its own modus operandi will be needed, *required*, as remedy to the breakdown of discipline that it has provoked. In (Puritan) America, in theory one can never be disciplined *enough.*

"A Horrible Case of Bestiality": "And after the time of the writing of these things befell a very sad accident of the like foul nature in this government, this very year, which I shall now relate. There was a youth whose name was Thomas Granger. He was servant to an honest man of Duxbury, being about 16 or 17 years of age. (His father and mother lived at the same time at Scituate.) He was this year detected of buggery, and indicted for the same, with a mare, a cow, two goats, five sheep, two calves and a turkey. Horrible it is to mention, but the truth of the history requires it. He was first discovered by one that accidentally saw his lewd practice towards the mare. (I forbear particulars). Being upon it examined and committed, in the end he not only confessed the fact with that beast at that time, but sundry times before and at several times with all the rest of the forenamed in his indictment. And this his free confession was not only in private to the magistrates (though at first he strived to deny it) but to sundry, both ministers and others; and afterwards, upon his indictment, to the whole Court and jury; and confirmed it at his execution. And whereas some of the sheep could not be so well known by his description of them, others with them were brought before him and he declared which were they and which were not. And accordingly he was cast by the jury and condemned, and after executed about the 8th of September, 1642. A very sad spectacle it was. For first the mare and then the cow and the rest of the lesser cattle were killed before his face, according to the law, Levicticus xx.15; and then he himself was executed. The cattle were all cast into a great and large pit that was digged for purpose of them, and no use made of any part of them.

Upon the examination of this person and also of a former that had made some sodomitical attempts upon another, it being demanded of them how they came first to the knowledge and practice of such wickedness, the one confessed he had long used it in old England; and this youth last spoken of said he was taught it by another that had heard of such things from some in England when he was there, and they kept cattle together. By which it appears how one wicked person may infect many, and what care all ought to have what servants they bring into their families."

How to do justice to the violence of this passage, its *horror*, a passage from 1642, but an historical moment that has echoed through the centuries? How to do justice to its grotesque righteousness, its *perversion*?

How much virtue can a society stand? Puritanism: a *loving* morality that kills, that cannibalizes its own . . .

Within the Puritan ethos, there is no privacy; everything must be transparent before God, and before his elect so that they can preserve His kingdom, root out failure, and *punish* it . . . punishment being the chief means of protecting a godliness, which, oddly, is seen as vulnerable, oddly fragile . . .

The private is the domain of sin; the public is the domain in which sin is identified, exposed and punished. The public domain in the New World: less an arena to do good; more, an arena in which the extirpation of evil takes place . . .

The Puritan body: something *alien*, something to destroy, something to sacrifice. When the Aztecs made human sacrifices, cut out still-beating hearts, it was done to acknowledge the power and value of the human body (as well as the power of one body over another); when the Puritans sacrificed Thomas Granger, the act expresses a disgust toward the human body itself, a desire to be free of its corruptions.

For the Puritans at Plymouth, sins cannot simply be *generally* known and understood; they have to be known in detail: examined minutely, studied, picked over, classified, catalogued—ultimately arranged to fit a taxonomy of sinfulness. In a Puritan culture, sins are fetishized more than virtue (think of *Paradise Lost*). Sinfulness is scrutinized in order to remind the elect of godliness, yet the obsession with it ultimately means that they bleed into one another, and virtue always comes to carry the taint of sinfulness . . .

The obsession with detailing sexual taboos transforms the readers of its legal-theological texts into sexual voyeurs. All discussions of sexuality become pornographic as sexual detail is pressed into the service of moral judgment. Puritanism *produces* the deviancy it is scandalized by; indeed, Puritanism is addicted to scandal, particularly sexual scandal. Scandal: the Great Legitimizer . . .

The confessional imperative: desire arraigned before the Law. Desire is forced to declare its own turpitude, to deny itself. It is important that the condemnation be initiated by the perpetrator (there not being the prohibition against self-incrimination) so that the judicial system can escape responsibility for its judgment: it must be a *free* confession . . .

Thomas Granger was killed because his acts of bestiality proved the animal nature of humans, proved *our* animality, and thus threw into question the view that humans are not animals, but above them as God is above us (a truth buried in Bradford's pit).

The ritualistic cruelty of the Pilgrims: "For first the mare and then the cow and the rest of the lesser cattle were killed before his face, according to the law, Leviticus xx.15; and then he himself was executed. A cruelty calculated to produce horror, as Granger is compelled to watch the execution of the animals with which had mated . . . after which he is executed and buried with them. The desire expressed here on the part of the Puritans is to *bury* the sexual contagion—not just the contagion of bestiality, but all sexuality—to stamp it out, to contain it, to kill it. A witch hunt against the irrepressible . . .

For the Puritans, sexuality had an essentially *theological* importance. It had no independent status: it signified either godliness or ungodliness—but given its ungovernable self-interest, even its godliness was suspect.

Granger's abuse of the animals is turned into a legal-theological *spectacle* that involves open legal proceedings, the courts, a jury, judicial judgment, grisly public executions. Why? To make him an example, but also an outcast, one who has made himself not merely unclean, but *inhuman* as a consequence of his actions, a loss of humanity signified by his burial with the animals he molested. The desire is to symbolically link Granger with deviancy, expel it, and through that sacrifice, re-establish the purity of Plymouth Plantation. Take note of the *ferocity* of the desire for purity— and the complex, ruthless systems they devised for the protection of it . . .

At the same time, *Of Plymouth Plantation* expresses an immense anxiety about purity: the Pilgrims have to trace the *source* of the contagion, and they have to find that source outside themselves. Evil must always originate outside the godly—to think otherwise, approaches the border of the unthinkable . . .

The purity of the land is insisted upon in part because it is the palimpsest upon which God's will—and temperament—is written. It is the book of

God, and for the Pilgrims, God's will is signified, first and foremost, in the world's motions: "This year, about the first or second of June, was a great and fearful earthquake. It was in this place heard before it was felt. It came with a rumbling noise or low murmur, like unto remote thunder. It came from the northward and passed southward, as the noise approached nearer, the earth began to shake and came at length with that violence as caused platters, dishes and suchlike things as stood upon the shelves, to clatter and fall down. Yea, persons were afraid of the houses themselves. It so fell out that at the same time divers of the chief of this town were met together at one house, conferring with some of their friends that were upon their removal from the place, as if the Lord would hereby show the signs of His displeasure, in their shaking a-pieces and removals one from another. However, it was very terrible for the time, and as the men were set talking in the house, some women and others were without the doors, and the earth shook with that violence as they could not stand without catching hold of the posts and pales that stood next them. But the violence lasted not long. And about half an hour, or less came another noise and shaking, but neither so loud nor strong as the former, but quickly passed over and so it ceased. It was not only on the seacoast, but the Indians felt it within land, and some ships that were upon the coast were shaken by it. So powerful is the mighty hand of the Lord, as to make both the earth and sea to shake, and the mountains to tremble before Him, when He pleases. And who can stay his hand?"

The moral? That God shows his displeasure over the dispersal of Plymouth Plantation by afflicting the land with an earthquake? More important than the actual message signified by the earthquake is the interpretive compulsion it manifests. The compulsion to discern a theological meaning in nature is everywhere in Puritan writing, but observe the need to always speak *for* others—for God, for the earth, for the Indians, never to allow them to speak for themselves, never to allow *difference* to impinge, to trouble the unitary language! Difference itself for the Puritans always smacked of the unredeemed, if not the Satanic. And the New World itself is only tolerable once it is converted into a stage for the enactment and discernment of God's meaning; as God's elect, the Pilgrims too write *over* the land, seeking to subsume its vastness and heterogeneity, its wealth of unrecognizable signs, within the narrow margins of an Old World, bookish, theological language . . .

That experience always has a *moral*—the curse of the Puritan inheritance ...

The end of the New Jerusalem. What brought about the demise of Plymouth Plantation? Its end was assured when the cold, material assessment of the land outweighed the moral, metaphysical one, when the land became something to own rather than to *redeem*: "For now as their stocks increased and the increase vendible, there was no longer any holding them together, but now they must of necessity go to their great lots. They could not otherwise keep their cattle, and having oxen grown they must have land for plowing and tillage. And no man now thought he could live except he had cattle and a great deal of ground to keep them, all striving to increase their stocks. By which means they were scattered all over the Bay quickly and the town in which they lived compactly till now was left very thin and in a short time almost desolate." Ultimately, the paradise of material accumulation proved to be more seductive than the collective, theocratic vision of the land as a New Jerusalem.

The building of paradise can withstand disease, division, death, intrigue and starvation—but never prosperity.

(Bradford's Book of Books records a paradise lost—with no *understanding* of it. Yet read right, it prophesies the future of the New World, a future which enacts again and again, the loss of paradise, each time a new event without precedent, each time a silent catastrophe that impugns the power of words . . .)

Chapter 2
Melville and Bartleby:
Facing the End of Audience

"Everything stated or expressed by man is a note
in the margin of a completely erased text."
—Fernando Pessoa

What can we face? The face as cipher, sign, image. 'Bartleby' stages the terrible mystery of faces, the equally terrible mystery of our own. Facing it, face offs, to turn one's face to the wall, to lose face, to gain it. The tragedy of each is the tragedy of all . . .

The worker consents—or he faces death (quickly or slowly). This is Bartleby's recognition. But in consenting, ironically, he also faces death, the death of the self. It doesn't matter that the self is a fiction. In fact, the murder of the fictive self, the self that finds a place within society, that has basked in social approval, is more tortuous and painful than the death of any actual self. This is what it means to "lose face."

Becoming a pariah is one thing; becoming exiled from who you thought you once were is another. Or is Bartleby's slow, deliberate journey of self-exile a journey to freedom? Freedom has significance only in relation to a context: freedom to one is not freedom to another. So: Heaven has levels, degrees, and degrees of separation.

The slow sad spectacle of the self, the monad, staging its own death for an audience that doesn't exist.

Or it exists, but cannot clap: it has not yet found the means to look about and see that the drama is *in* the clapping, not just the performance, the one loud roar of approval that sweeps aside both the past and the future.

Freedom from external restraint, unto death. "Freedom-from" versus "freedom-in": in this most free of nations, there is no freedom-in being. Your freedom is guaranteed by the right to die by yourself, with whatever self you can covet, unencumbered by love or relation. Few would dream of curtailing that freedom. Bartleby: the nineteenth-century ancestor to every homeless person wandering aimlessly on America's streets, each one the sovereign of all he surveys.

Bartleby never *argued* with anyone; he never tried to prove a point, win converts, vanquish foes. What does this lack of rhetorical aggression signify? The fruitlessness of conversion via argumentation? The failure of rhetoric? The contamination of rhetoric by a culture in which most "disinterested" expressions cloak naked self-interest? Bartleby's "I prefer not to" exists as an assertion of will—but not will-to-truth.

The most destructive of all faces: benign tolerance. This is the face of Bartleby's employer. It disguises its own intolerance within a mask of benevolence. Worse: because that intolerance cannot be admitted, it does not exist. And because it does not exist, it is free to become pitiless.

Behind the narrator's courteousness, theatricalized benevolence and good manners lurks the threat of violence, social violence. Without these rhetorical forms, manners, forms of self-presentation, capitalist society would be undressed, its violence made manifest. With them, it is dressed up as civilized, moral, benevolent. Bartleby forces it to undress; he forces it to endure the shame of exposure, the danger of self-recognition. Society takes its *revenge* upon Bartleby.

About Bartleby, the narrator says, "no materials exist, for a full and satisfactory biography of this man." In being unknown and unknowable, Bartleby exists as a threat to society's will-to-know, to narrative itself. That which is un-narratable *must* be narrated, must be known.

Everyone, everything must be faced, categorized, reported upon. To be unknown and unknowable is to incur the wrath of custom and law which demands a *modest* amount of submission.

Those about "whom nothing is ascertainable" defy the order of things, which rests on the ability to recognize, ascertain, assess. One death meets another.

"What my own astonished eyes saw of Bartleby, *that* is all I know of him." Astonishment polices reality: it turns it into heaven or hell. Hell is what is unrecognizable; heaven is only a name for what can be recognized.

To trade in "bonds" "mortgages" and "title deeds" is to trade in articles of possession. Within this world, language—writing—becomes the guarantor of ownership. The language of the law attempts to contain the irreducible play of meaning in language by means of complete discrimination, complete description. Through exactitude and precision it attempts to forestall all contingency, all unforeseen contexts. Bartleby's refusal to yield his soul defies a social order possessed by the desire to possess everything and to translate its own imperial ambition into an idiom of benevolence and generosity.

The soul is what is withheld; the soul is that which is proffered *without being acknowledged as such*. It is then material and invisible. The achievement of Bartleby is that he maintains, in large part, the invisibility of his soul. This too is his tragedy; it is also the tragedy of the society that demands it.

What is safety in a world made "safe" by money? The mansion becomes the mausoleum.

"Poetic enthusiasm" will always be an embarrassment in the face of prudence and method. Prudence—thou knows not what thou art!

In a society in which the lack of "poetic enthusiasm" is judged to be good, any evidence of it will be seen as a weakness, a failure of restraint.

Wall Street: even the name is mythological: destiny materialized within the flux of numbers rising or falling on the stock exchange. The market depends upon fluctuation, but fluctuation within limits. Wall Street creates walls—as well as the need for them. It also creates a demand for a limit to tolerance. In a market society, tolerance *must* be limited else there will be no profit. To be infinitely tolerant, that is, to be meaningfully tolerant, would require unending expenditure. Thus in market societies, tolerance becomes a most precious commodity; its value is dependent upon it being "cashed in" only rarely.

In 1653, Wall Street was named for a "barricade built by Peter Stuyveysant to protect the early Dutch settlers from the local Indians" (Peter Geisst, *Wall Street: A History*). Wall Street has always been, then, a place of barricades, an instrument of separation, a means to distance "entrepreneurial" settlers from the locals, a place of appropriation and exploitation. Indeed, it marks a border, a boundary, a space designed to produce both wealth and alienation. It marks a frontier; a defensive establishment already prepared against the backlash of the people beyond it. It thus exists as a predatory commercial site, though so "normalized" it virtually ceases to look or feel like one. Necessarily, it is a place of self-righteousness; wealth must be a sign of God's favor. Yet there is uneasiness here too, rooted in the partially repressed recognition of the illegitimacy that comes from appropriation, which must always be legitimized. The aggressor must always be the victim.

Through his unorthodoxy, Bartleby challenges the liberal definition of benevolence. His employer, however, writes to convince us of his unsullied liberalism. The reader too is called upon to confirm the narrator's own skewed self-image. In doing so, Melville shows the insecurity of the liberal mind—and its monstrosity. The entire world exists to confirm it in its essential benevolence. But since at some level it *knows* that it is not benevolent, the world exists to prop up a tattered fiction. Everything is sacrificed. The liberal mind: pitiless, egotistical, endlessly benign, endlessly serene.

Wall Street is presented to us as dialectic of "industry and life" by day and "emptiness" and "vacancy" by night. Bartleby shows, by contrast, the emptiness and vacancy of industry itself. Even to the narrator, Wall Street is a "Petra" and a ruined "Carthage."

To blot a document for a scrivener is a mortal sin, for it reminds the reader that the law is not a distant, Olympian arbiter of right and wrong, but a frail, imperfect human institution . . . lawyers, not surprisingly, want to exorcise all blots form their records. As if the law could be unblemished.

The impertinence of Bartleby: he does not *negotiate* the terms of his employment; he decides and acts off his own bat. Despite his mildness, his is the grossest form of insubordination. Subordinates who take their own preferences in hand and follow them up challenge the legitimacy of authority. Thus the latent, nearly extinguished utopianism of "Bartleby": what would be if all the wretched of the earth declared "I prefer not to"?

Bartleby alone appears to be self-conscious, undeceived. This degree of self-awareness renders him unfit for labor which depends, to varying degrees, upon a dimming of self-knowledge, self-consciousness. Within American capitalism, self-knowledge brings the individual to a state of unfreedom. Its price: exile. To be self-conscious in America is to become an exile, a social outcast. Individualism becomes the compensatory myth for a society intolerant of it.

What is the black wall that Bartleby sees through his windowpanes? It is nothing but sheer blankness, Necessity, the limitation that he endures, the sum of limitations upon individual desire by the rule of law and social custom. It is the pitilessness of all laws, written and unwritten, that demand conformity and obedience. It is the primal scene of socialization in which the implacable order of things confronts human desire with its all—too—human face.

To write the law over and over again, to copy it repeatedly, is to perform the individual's subjection to the law: he is embodying it within language, enabling it to take material form; he is giving it his life force. The scrivener is not writing the law; it is writing itself through him. It is impervious to death and decay; the scrivener, by contrast, is mortal, temporal, frail, corruptible. The scrivener embodies the fate of the subject: to be subjected to the law is to be its subject. Which is synonymous with being subject-less. The irony of Melville's parable: fleeing the death of the subject only *hastens* it.

The labor of the scrivener: writing without thinking, writing that faithfully and mindlessly duplicates the signifier, writing that has as its sole object the *reproduction* of the word of law—is this not a symbol of the labor of the intellectual working under the aegis of an anti-individualistic capitalism?

Bartleby arrives at his employer's premises as an adult, but an adult without a history. It is this emptiness, this lack of a knowable past, the silence of his past, his solitude and lack of connection that distinguishes him, paradoxically, as history's subject. His silence about his past only amplifies that untold drama. That past, that history, becomes too monumental to be written. It is unrepresentable, but in becoming unrepresentable, it acquires a ghostly presence. History haunts Bartleby. It is unseen but everywhere it makes itself felt with its uncanny presence. (Bartleby too becomes a wraith).

Bartleby is *stricken* with life, with the burden of living.

Why does Bartleby begin his employment with an orgy of productivity? To obliterate the past? To identify himself with social expectation in a failed attempt to conform? The reasons are unknowable, perhaps to himself as well as Melville. *That* is respect for fiction.

Alternatively: Bartleby's orgy of productivity at the beginning of his employment is the sign of the unconsciousness responding to the demands of everyday life. Bartleby's frenzy mimics the law of productivity, becoming a grotesque parody of it. To live as a conformist is to live as a parody, to live as a mimic man. Bartleby prefers to live as a grotesque rather than to live as a parody.

For Bartleby's employer as for most representatives of the law, civil disobedience— "I prefer not to"— is a species of madness. In Paradise, refusal has always been a form of heresy, of madness. "What right do you have to reject Eden, my Eden"? (Even Ginger Nut thinks Bartleby is "luny").

For Bartleby, "reason" is unreason. Its tyranny is met by mildness, mildness that exists as reproach, gentle condemnation, a refusal to enter into the ugly economy of compulsion. Bartleby's mildness, then, is utopian—or at least a faint sign of the utopian in a world degraded by imperatives. By contrast, Turkey affirms his employer's rules "with submission."

Bartleby is regarded by his employer as unreasonable, the very embodiment of unreason. What Bartleby forces us to see is that reason is a fiction authored by certain interests (the legal profession, the middle class, etc) in order to legitimize themselves. Reason, of course, is always what you have but the other person does not. Since the Enlightenment, reason has been deified as Truth, but in so doing it betrays its own idealization. That which cannot be proven wrong becomes, by definition, an article of faith. We should speak of *reasons* rather than Reason. In actual practice, Reason has little to do with itself.

"Come forth and do your duty "declares Bartleby's employer to Bartleby. Duty: every society induces it in order to ensure its own reproduction. Duty is needed to overcome the inevitable revulsion toward the menial, the abhorrent, as well as the mundane. Doing one's duty always involves an annihilation of the self—as well as a fulfillment of it.

Without irony, the master looks to the slave for confirmation of his essential benevolence; similarly, the employer demands of his employee that he confirm his employer's sense of tolerance and benevolence. The annoyance Bartleby's employer feels toward Bartleby is, if anything, exceeded by the irritation the other scriveners feel toward Bartleby for "shirking" his work. Turkey and Nipper's inflamed response to Bartleby's *non serviam*— "Shall I go and black out his eyes" —expresses the narrator's own rage against Bartleby, a rage he cannot express himself inasmuch as it would give the lie to his own magnanimity. But it also allows him to act the role of the liberal, long-suffering employer (which, in truth, he is). 'Bartleby' thus explores the psychic organization of labor under capitalism in which the wage earner expresses the anger and frustrations of his boss, which also become *his*. Melville reveals a system in which one class not only exploits another, but it also expects the exploited class to voice the angers, the frustrations, and the point of view of the dominant class, here, the middle class. For Melville, this system is essentially two-faced. The question of voice or *expression* (the representation of what is internal) then becomes immensely fraught, caught up in the unconscious social imperative to speak for interests that are *not* one's own. In part this explains Bartleby's linguistic miserliness: to speak more would be to invite his speech to be infected by the speech and interests of another class. Bartleby's linguistic minimalism resists this enforced, class-based ventriloquism.

Failing to reform Bartleby, his employer takes it upon himself to read Bartleby's protest as an opportunity to exercise his own moral improvement. That he fails is not a sign of his moral turpitude but a sign that moral improvement in a Puritan society is impossible.

Bartleby repossesses his employer's premises. He has a fine indifference for property. Is it any wonder he must die?

"Immediately then the thought came sweeping across me, what miserable friendlessness and loneliness are here revealed." To have his life interpreted for us by one with such suspect motives: this is Bartleby's fate and that of all the dispossessed. He cannot narrate his own life, tell his own story in his own words. In Melville's America, identity is not something you simply have or own; it is something largely conferred upon you by others. Identity is a function of how you are seen. In a society possessed by the drama of individualism, the social rears its ugly head by silently and efficiently forging an identity for everyone, an identity that is never wholly available for inspection and understanding *by* the individual. The American self: one who thinks he knows himself utterly.

Spectre, spectator, specimen: Bartleby cannot escape the imprisonment of categories, more carceral than mortar.

The narrator says he feels a "bond of a common humanity" with Bartleby, yet his actions do not acknowledge the sanctity of any such bond. This then is the fate of the liberal mind: to feel one thing, but to have that feeling, that liberal sentiment, overborne by the "more practical" demands of class and the conformities a market society exacts.

"Pallid," "miserable," "silent,", "pale", "cadaverously gentlemanly": Bartleby is not only deathly in appearance; he *is* death. Death to social convention, death to social custom, to normative expectation, to social behavior. Negating social expectation, Bartleby is negated. That is, he becomes more like who he *is*. He approaches the horizon of his identity, which is paradoxically nothing as well as being the unspeakable form of his resistance to social law. This is why the narrator pities him, hates him, loves him. As an object of pity, Bartleby's unspoken critique of everything that narrator stands for (professionalism, class, respectability, tolerance, etc.) does not have to be engaged. Indeed, once made an object of pity, his unspoken condemnation can be dismissed as eccentricity or lunacy.

The laws of employment permit all kinds of plunder, invasion, appropriation. Because the narrator observes that Bartleby's desk "is mine," it too can be penetrated by him. He has in law, if not in ethics, a right to rifle Bartleby's desk. The narrator possesses a will-to-truth vis-a-vis Bartleby: his mysteriousness, his reserve, his enigmatic taciturn character *must* be made explicable. That it is not defies the narrator's complacently bourgeois worldview, which demands attribution, causal hermeneutics, simplicity, clarity. Bartleby gives this will-to-truth, which is also a will-to-power, no relief. What knowledge cannot know it must dismiss, pity or delegitimize as contemptible or as a mere object of curiosity.

Bartleby: the exemplary American. He tries—and fails—to make a home for himself within the ever-mutating, ever-the-same precincts of capitalism and ends up being imprisoned by it.

Of deadwall reveries: ". . . standing in one of those deadwall reveries of his." The reverie, long the ally of American self-invention, self-fashioning, can also be its undoing, especially when reverie becomes a substitute for doing. Bartleby is Benjamin Franklin's nemesis, the presence of a horrific lack of productivity in American culture that Franklin sought to annihilate, or at least, shame out of existence. The narrator (Benjamin Franklin's alter ego in the story) initially feels pity for Bartleby, a pity that transmogrifies into revulsion. It is not only that Bartleby represents an entirely different principle of living; it is that he cannot be changed to be in alignment with the narrator's complacent establishment values ("What I saw that morning persuaded me that the scrivener was the victim of an innate and incurable disorder"). Hence, Bartleby must be cast out.

The initial test of Bartleby's excommunication will be whether he will divulge the particulars of his deliberately veiled history. If he refuses to do so, the narrator is determined to fine him. Significantly, he is *not* first asked to become more efficient. He is asked to reveal his soul, to become transparent before the gaze of his employer, to lose his identity as a separate, equal and distinctive life, indeed to lose his private history. He is asked, in short, to become a case, an aggregate of facts, an object of narration, a known story, an *employee* instead of an individual. To the question, "Will you tell me anything about yourself?," Bartleby responds "I would prefer not to."

Bartleby's presence, his example, is a contagion that must be contained. Within the highly conventionalized world of employer-employee relations, preference cannot be allowed to have much more than a rhetorical significance. Preference speaks to individual will, which in Melville's America, exists only ideologically, or at the level of enunciation. Individual will haunts America, its brick and mortar office buildings, its devil-deal with Wall Street, its boom times and its bust ones; it is dead but its uneasy spirit is everywhere, a reminder of what has been lost, or perhaps what once was envisioned but never realized.

In the face of society's "thou must," Bartleby heroically maintains his own sense of will. He cannot be bribed to conform; he will not acknowledge the coercion of politeness, the ascendancy of manners. Yet he is not free. Obedience to social law and defiance it are seen by Melville to be equally constraining. Defying social law defines Bartleby, almost absolutely. Wherever he turns there are walls. Bartleby is an individual who cannot free himself from his narrator, even from his author. Melvillean tragedy: narration itself as a form of subjection, unless the reader rewrites the story . . .

Self-interest too dictates the ultimate removal of Bartleby from the narrator's law offices; the narrator decides he cannot afford generosity beyond the recognized border of conventional liberalism: the silent uncooperative presence of Bartleby has begun to affect his "professional reputation." In a society actuated in the main by the profit motive, self-interest will always be the cardinal value; other pretenders exist, but none command the same degree of allegiance.

What earthly right do you have to stay here? Do you pay any rent? Do you pay my taxes? Or is this property yours?" In nineteenth-century America, as now, in practice rights are guaranteed by money and property not by "higher" ethical, legal or constitutional principles. Melville's postmortem on the body politic reveals not so much a divide between ethical and political life but a conquest of ethical principles by capitalist premises such that thinking beyond them requires an immense act of the imagination. By 1854, the "cash-payment nexus" had settled America; the only space outside it was the space of the imagination. The great achievement of capitalism is that it forces its dissidents and critics into exile, it forces us to inhabit the territory of the imagination, which it then de-legitimizes as unreal, as mythical, a place of childish fantasy, a land of improbability. From whence will come the beast, slouching towards Bethlehem.

Horror—that Bartleby should dispossess his employer. He worries that "... in the end [he might] perhaps outlive me, and claim possession of my office by right of his perpetual occupancy." Fear of dispossession leads to dispossession. Fear the devil! Possession, the devil! Legitimacy, the devil!

From valued employee to recalcitrant employee to enigma to apparition: by the end of the story Bartleby is made to metamorphose again: in a final incarnation he is seen to be an "intolerable incubus." This is no exaggeration; he *is* an incubus. He haunts the living by his mere *being*. Merely *being* uncooperative becomes an affront to bourgeois propriety, to professional decorum, to normativity itself. Bartleby becomes burdened with the socially unsaid in America, particularly the gap between our idealistic image of the American body politic and the harsher reality. Bartleby is—worst sin of all—an embarrassment. He embarrasses the narrator's notion of himself as a generous individual; he embarrasses society's pretense to be a society in which action is grounded in principle. His mere presence *mocks* the American claim to have established a uniquely free polity.

"Bartleby" is about the magical power, the horrific power, of representation to transform lives. The narrator defines Bartleby's life; his definition of Bartleby as an outsider, an "intolerable incubus," becomes material, actual, in the body of Bartleby, wraithlike in prison, by the wall, awaiting death. In representing others as inhuman, supernatural, mythical, fantastic, they *are* metamorphosed into fiends, spirits, ghosts, devils, diseases, witches. Via this magic they can be annihilated, burned, slaughtered, converted, exorcised, chained, imprisoned, starved and mocked—made to gabble, made to flee, made to fly.

Once Bartleby's employer deserts his law offices, he is finally able to separate himself from any sense of responsibility to Bartleby. But his departure does not signify a new disavowal of Bartleby, only the acting out of a disavowal that has already taken place. The disavowal merely becomes visible, public, as he makes clear to the new occupant of his former premises on Wall Street: "I am very sorry, sir, said I, with assured tranquility, but an inward tremor, "but really the man you allude to is nothing to me—he is no relation or apprentice of mine, that you should hold me responsible for him." What *fear* there is here—fear of a social contract that would bind one individual to another, make one responsible to another, or merely genuinely responsive to another. Bartleby's employer is desperate that he not be made "responsible for him." He expresses a horror toward social responsibility. 'Bartleby' is in this sense a dramatization of the American horror toward the notion of the social as the environment in which individual destiny receives completion. It ironizes—despairingly! —the narrator's desire for the social to be replaced by an environment in which individuals pursue their ambitions limited only by the pressures of economic necessity, class, and a legal system firmly rooted in the prerogatives of wealth and property.

Within this vision, the social makes no demands on individuals vis-à-vis other ones, and should not. It is a space populated only by a single individual and his solipsistic ambitions. Yet the emptiness of this social space demands the most rigorous policing. It must not be filled up, certainly not by a vision of the social as fulfilling. The social is defined by Melville as the space of the prison yard, demarcated by "the surrounding walls, of amazing thickness."

Ironically, in so privatizing the dream of the social as a source of support and enrichment, the social domain actually is reduced to becoming barren, coercive and exploitative. Melville's irony: horror at the horror we have allowed the social to become.

"As I afterwards learned, the poor scrivener, when told that he must be conducted to the Tombs, offered not the slightest obstacle, but, in his pale, unmoving way, silently acquiesced." The shameless of false pity, false piety! Bartleby acquiesces in the face of death. Pity is death too—in this sense, Bartleby's removal to the Tombs is merely the actualization of the living death that he has already endured. Bartleby faces this fate without flinching. He acquiesces not only because he knows his end is inevitable, but because it is the ineluctable fulfillment of the social law, of social life. (To say that the social does not exist in 'Bartleby' would be to simplify and to miss a finer irony. The social exists—but it exists in its purest form only negatively, punitively; it exists as a coercive power applied to those who violate the law of unfettered individualism or the law that sanctifies existence as a process of accumulation).

Bartleby is imprisoned as a way punishing him for resisting the dictates of individualism. The strongest social taboo in Melville's America is a taboo against thinking beyond the narrow confines of individualism. If you cannot live as an individual conforming to a liberal worldview, then you will die as something unrecognized: a true individual. Whether or not you *want* to conform then becomes a superannuated consideration.

In refusing to become an object of his employer's gaze, Bartleby becomes an object of the gaze of murderers and thieves. His dissident behavior renders him lower than that of the lowest of criminals. How ironic that this most private of individuals should suffer the indignity of having his privacy stripped away, made an object of curiosity, a spectacle for the amusement of society's outcasts (who only violated the letter, not the spirit of the law). Glassed in, he lives under the gaze of society's condemned; his unrecorded sentence is to suffer the loss of privacy endlessly. Having defied the imperatives of materialistic individualism, he is made to endure a degraded and grotesque sociality. This is his "freedom." And in giving him the run of the prison, society can be persuaded of its own generosity. "Being under no disgraceful charge, and quite serene and harmless in all his ways, they had permitted him freely to wander about the prison, and especially, in the inclosed grass-platted yards thereof. And so I found him there, standing all alone in the quietest of the yards, his face towards a high wall, while all around, from the narrow slits of the jail windows, I thought I saw peering out upon him the eyes of murderers and thieves."

Bartleby is never charged with any crime; to charge him with one would be to face the unacknowledgeable, the brutality of the unwritten law of individualism. He is, indeed, "under no disgraceful charge."

Bartleby's face is "toward a high wall," the wall of Necessity, the wall of repression, the wall of the law that condemns Bartleby. Bartleby can see it; he knows what it is. Little wonder that when he's saluted by his former employer who visits him in the Tombs, Bartleby replies "'I know you,' he said, without looking around—'and I want nothing to say to you.'"

And the falseness of his former employer's response! 'It was not I that brought you here, Bartleby,' said I, keenly pained at his implied suspicion. 'And to you, this should not be so vile a place. Nothing reproachful attaches to you by being here. And see, it is not so sad a place as one might think. Look, there is the sky, and here is the grass.'" The narrative voice smoothly defines reality. There is no presumption in this—for he belongs to that class which *has* defined reality. For those who do not have to live with the falseness of representation, hell can be all the heaven there is to know.

But there is falseness here, falseness based on an invincible form of self-deceit. While the narrator did not technically remove Bartleby from his premises, his own behavior made that all but inevitable. The narrator will not face his complicity in bringing Bartleby to this end. He will not accept responsibility for it, or for his own actions; his is the voice of individualism: not thou but I! His rhetoric transforms himself into a martyr to Bartleby's unwarranted and unjust suspicion; likewise, it makes a heaven of hell.

In the narrator's last attempt to convert Bartleby to accept the world as it is, he encourages Bartleby to accept the "grub-man" in the Tombs as his servant. Bartleby rejects the role of master just as he rejected the role of servant.

Bartleby's emaciated, wraith-like body symbolizes his lack of visibility, his social invisibility. Bartleby is out of bounds, beyond the narrator's ability to recognize him. Why then eat? What is there to eat? Eating exists as a form of hopefulness. It expresses a sense of hope about the future, or at least the belief that the future will be responsive to individual human desire. What is there to sustain Bartleby? His frail body records the cost of defying the social law, which enshrines mastery and slavery as society's *modus vivendi*. He becomes —-another— invisible man.

"'Deranged? Deranged is it? Well, now, upon my word, I thought that friend of yourn was a gentleman forger; they are always pale and genteel-like, them forgers. I can't help pity 'em—can't help it, sir.'" This, the grub man to the narrator, about Bartleby at the story's end. Forgers pass off fake documents as "authentic" originals. Forgers thus exist as the doppelganger to scriveners. Scriveners produce copies, but copies recognized *as* copies. Their copies do not destabilize this economy of authenticity; indeed they affirm it. Bartleby's refusal to work is also a refusal to work as a scrivener, as a worker who supports this economy of authenticity. Has not the law forged itself? Has it not declared itself authentic—indeed the source of authentic behavior for the body politic? Doesn't the law's excessively punitive stance toward forgery betray its own anxiety about its own "authenticity," its own insecurity about its status as the embodiment of transcendent truths about justice? Doesn't Bartleby's wasted body declare the inauthenticity of the law, and the inauthenticity of the lawyer-narrator who presumes to narrate Bartleby's life?

"Dead letters! does it not sound like dead men? Conceive a man by nature and misfortune prone to a pallid hopelessness, can any business seem more fitted to heighten it than by continually handling these dead letters, and assorting them for the flames. For by the cart-load they are annually burned. Sometimes from out the folded paper the pale clerk takes a ring-the finger it was meant for, perhaps, moulders in the grave; a bank note sent in swiftest charity—he whom it would relieve, nor eats nor hungers any more; pardon for those who died despairing; hope for those who died unhoping; good tidings for those who died stifled by unrelieved calamities. On errands of life, these letters speed to death. Ah, Bartleby! Ah, humanity!"

The fact that the narrator—the agent of Bartleby's destruction—is also his elegist is a sign of the text's veiled outlook, for it signifies either the first shoots of change—or the final cruelty of the dream of a New Jerusalem in the New World.

"Bartleby the Scrivener" is composed of dead letters—the dead letter of the law; the dead letters of a constitutional democracy; the death of individualism; the death of narrative's power to transform social failure; the death of authenticity and benevolence; in a sense, the death of humanity. Just as dead letters are letters sent too late to those who were despairing, and now are dead, so too 'Bartleby' is a dead letter sent to a reading public, which by accepting, indeed internalizing, compromised versions of freedom and community, takes on the greenish tint of death.

But the letter itself, like the letters Bartleby consigned to the flames, is also charged with redemptive energy, with the desire to redeem loss and failure. The irony is inescapable: redemption for those who are beyond it. The imperative is to look at the death-face of the American body politic face on, to see it in all of its ghastly pallor. Seeing—recognition—is the necessary prerequisite for social transformation. Melville's text is haunted by loss, by almost-extinguished hopes. Hauntings terrorize, but they may also be quests for redemption. Just as it awaits a general resurrection of all dead letters, Melville's text awaits, still, its audience.

Chapter 3
Ghost Writing:
Whitman's *Specimen Days*

Everything is again set in motion—called into question—by writing.
—Edmond Jabès

Specimen Days: Whitman's back-pocket journal of his experiences during the Civil War—always the smear of history that runs across the page, always the trace of it in the slant of the sentences, in the folded sheets of paper, the lightest pencil strokes, the blood stains that threaten to blot out the words . . .

Specimen Days: not an iron-willed, seamless narrative, but a deliberately fragmented one, whose very fragmentariness longs to enter more deeply into experience. *Specimen Days* wills itself into being as a miscellany of observations, "blood smutch'd" pages torn from the notebook of experience, "diary scraps and memoranda," "a bundle," which acknowledges in its own rough fragmentariness the weight of history— and the lightness and fragility—the *partiality*—of the paper upon which experience gets scratched out in letters.

Specimen Days: A book that would remake the world in its own image.

Death sentences: "I commenced at the close of 1862, and continued steadily through '63, '64 and '65, to visit the sick and wounded of the army both on the field and in the hospitals in and around Washington city. From the first I kept little note-books for impromptu jottings in pencil, to refresh my memory of names and circumstances, and what was specially wanted, &c. In those I brief'd cases, persons, sights, occurrences in camp, by the bed-side, and not seldom by the corpses of the dead. Some were scratch'd down from narratives I heard and itemized while watching, or waiting, or tending somebody amid those scenes. I have dozens of such little-notebooks left, forming a special history of those years, for myself alone, full of associations, never to be possibly said or sung. I wish I could convey to the reader the associations that attach to these soil'd and creas'd livraisons, each composed of a sheet or two of paper, folded small to carry in the pocket, and fasten'd with a pin. I leave them just as I threw them by after the war, blotch'd here and there with more than one blood-stain, hurriedly written, sometimes at the clinique, not seldom among the excitement of uncertainty, or defeat, or of action, or getting ready for it, or a march. Most of the pages from 26 to 81 are verbatim copies of those lurid and blood smutch'd little note-books."

Held together by a pin: the pin that binds also allows each page its own integrity, its status as an object in its own right, pinned though it may be. This is not the book as a seamless whole, a unity of design that allows the whole to come into being at the cost of the part. What holds this miscellany together is only a bit of metal: the guarantor of the integrity of the fragment. It pierces the paper, the writing, *makes* it a notebook. This is a different idea of the book, in which the part is not subordinated to the whole; here the part—the fragment—is liberated from the tyranny of the whole; it is simply let *be*, in all of its suggestive incompletion, in all of its perfect incompletion. Yet the ghost of each sibling-fragment haunts the others . . . each recollected day is a specimen, a preserved moment, a moment reclaimed from oblivion. The days of most intense pleasure, the boyhood remembrances, are of equal importance with the days of most intense pain and grief: they are specimen moments, specimens of a life, specimens too of national life. "Only in fragments can we read the immeasurable totality." (Edmond Jabès)

Whence these memories? From an intensity of seeing . . . *Specimen Days* sacralizes *seeing, remembering, and writing*: it sees them as symbolic modes of knitting together the nation—and alternatives to the violence that is tearing it apart. But Whitman's text honors a non-triumphalist seeing, a non-triumphalist remembering, a non-triumphalist writing—as the only hope for the republic. Otherwise, we inhabit a republic that is blind, endlessly self-assured, endlessly right, endlessly righteous; one unbordered by truth . . .

The form of *Specimen Days* embodies a vision of national accord, in which the parts are given expressive freedom, whilst still resonating with one another. Separate, semi-autonomous, yet interconnected and mutually dependent upon one another, they describe a whole that is greater than the sum of its parts: a notebook for a republic to come. (How many American texts expend themselves upon this dream, the dream of a republic not yet in existence but not yet out of mind!)

Life sentences: *Specimen Days* is not morbid; indeed, it's remarkable for its openness, its spontaneity, its open-heartedness to the world as it is, its responsiveness to the world in its becoming, the lyricism of its minute unfoldings. Is there a *freer*, more joyous beginning to any book than this?: "*Down in the Woods, July 2d, 1882.*:—If I do it at all I must delay no longer. Incongruous and full of skips and jumps as is that huddle of diary-jottings, war-memoranda of 1862–'65, Nature notes of 1877–'81, with Western and Canadian observations afterwards, all bundled up and tied by a big string, the resolution and indeed mandate comes to me this day, this hour—(and what a day! what an hour just passing! the luxury of riant grass and blowing breeze, with all the shows of sun and sky and perfect temperature, never before so filling me body and soul)—to go home, untie the bundle, reel out diary scraps and memoranda, just as they are, large or small, one after another, into print-pages, and let the mélange's lackings and wants of connection take care of themselves. It will illustrate one phase of humanity anyhow; how few of life's days and hours (and they not by relative value or proportion, but by chance) are ever noted. Probably another point too, how we give long preparations for some object, planning and delving and fashioning, and then, when the actual hour for doing arrives, finds ourselves still quite unprepared, and tumble the thing together, letting hurry and crudeness tell the story better than fine work. At any rate, I obey my happy hour's command, which seems curiously imperative. May-be, if I don't do anything else, I shall send out the most wayward, spontaneous, fragmentary book ever printed." Charged with an irrepressible life force, these sentences arrive at an awareness of the ephemerality of beauty through an awareness of the proximity of death; death is needed to produce "life sentences." Life sentences are death sentences. Every sentence restlessly seeks its own end —as well as its own ends.

Specimen Days: a ferrying back and forth between fugitive presents and pasts, of boyhoods and adulthoods, of thens and nows . . . but also a ferrying back and forth between the world of experience and that of representation, of speaking and writing such that the worlds are seen as connected, traversed, leading to one another, even as they cross one another out. Writing cannot wholly take into itself the world—but it can travel to it, visit it: the world always already determines its symbols, if not their fashionings. Writing as a ferry, as a means of transit between points, between worlds, a means of transit that has as its end the discovery of *awe*. Awe—and the writing of awe: the supplement of loss in the face of loss: "Indeed, I have always had a passion for ferries; to me they afford inimitable, streaming, never-failing, living poems. The river and bay scenery, all about New York island, any time of a fine day—the hurrying, splashing sea-tides, the changing panorama of steamers, all sizes, often a string of big ones outward bound to distant ports—the myriads of white-sail'd schooners, sloops, skiffs, and marvelously beautiful yachts— the majestic sound boats as they rounded the Battery and came along towards 5, afternoon, eastward bound, the prospect off towards Staten Island, or down the Narrows, or the other way up the Hudson—what refreshment of spirit such sight and experiences gave me years ago (and many a time since)."

The printed word exists in a world of silence, isolate. The printed page is *of* the world, but apart from it. Impressed upon the paper of the page, the printed word belongs to the domain of silence. The irony of coming to apprehend the world of noise—the world of violence and war—through the world of silence, the world of print: "News of the attack upon fort Sumter and *the flag* at Charleston Harbor, S.C., was receiv'd in New York city late at night (13th April, 1861) and was immediately sent out in extras of the newspapers. I had been to the opera in Fourteenth street that night, and after the performance was walking down Broadway toward twelve o' clock, on my way to Brooklyn, when I heard in the distance the loud cries of the newsboys, who came presently tearing and yelling up the street, rushing from side to side even more furiously than usual. I brought an extra and cross'd to the Metropolitan hotel (Niblio's) where the great lamps were still brightly blazing, and, with a crowd of others, who gather'd impromptu, read the news, which was evidently authentic. For the benefit of some who had no papers, one of us read the telegram aloud, while all listen'd silently and attentively. No remark was made by any of the crowd, which had increas'd to thirty or forty, but all stood a minute or two, I remember, before they dispers'd. I can almost see them there now, under the lamps at midnight again." *Specimen Days* translates the world of war—a world of noise, of cries and whispers—back into the domain of silence to commemorate that which cannot be spoken. Reading: a way of approaching death, and its final silence.

"O day everlasting within ephemeral day." (Edmond Jabès)

Specimen Days: a text that is always approaching twelve o'clock, midnight, that is, a certain *time* (symbolized by midnight, April 13, 1861). *At that moment nothing changed; everything came into being.*

The printed word depends upon the space between the letters, the field of the page, the field of the past. Every word, every sentence, every book has ghosts, is haunted, depends upon that ghosting, those absences. "*I can almost see them there now, under the lamps at midnight again.*" These apparitions determine the apparition that is writing. All writing is ghost writing . . .

Battle of Bull Run, July 1861: The first shock of defeat on the Union side: "The sun rises, but shines not. The men appear, at first sparsely and shame-faced enough, then thicker, in the streets of Washington—appear in Pennsylvania avenue and on the steps and basement entrances. They come along in disorderly mobs, some in squads, stragglers, companies. Occasionally, a rare regiment, in perfect order, with its officers (some gaps, dead, the true braves) marching in silence, with lowering faces, stern, weary to sinking, all black and dirty, but every man with his musket, and stepping alive; but these are the exceptions."

The perfect order of the regiments, with the gaps of the fallen left intact, is a commemoration in motion, an elegy in action. To march in this way is to pay tribute to the fallen, to honor them and to offer a visible reminder of the cost of war. Is not *Specimen Days*, with all of its gaps, its regular irregularity, like this honorific marching? Is it not trying to gesture to the price war exacts upon the living and the dead? And is not every book like this—a defeat, but also a testament to the dead—without which the book would not be?

The sleeping and the dead: "Amid the deep excitement, crowds and motion, and desperate eagerness, it seems strange to see many, very many, of the soldiers sleeping— in the midst of all, sleeping sound. They drop down anywhere, on the steps of houses, up close by the basements or fences, on the sidewalk, aside on some vacant lot, and deeply sleep. A poor seventeen or eighteen year old boy lies there, on the stoop of a grand house; he sleeps so calmly, so profoundly. Some clutch their muskets firmly even in sleep. Some in squads; comrades, brothers, close together—and on them, as they lay, sulkily drips the rain." In their trance-like sleep, the soldiers resemble the forms of those fallen on the battlefield. Their presence transforms Washington into a nether world, a mausoleum populated by graceful stone effigies, a metropolis turned necropolis. One sleep recalls another: a prophetic dream of a republic soon to be overrun by death. (Would we make war if the dead of all our wars inhabited Washington as these men do? What then would war *rhetoric* look like, sound like?)

For Whitman, writing is not a form of violence, but a form of tenderness, indeed, ministry. It is a way of ministering to the afflicted, the living, the dying, even the dead. They speak through him. Through writing, he raises the dead, translates the broken language of the body, the language of despair and longing—the punctuation of a gesture—into written language, into the whisper of hope . . .

The power of *Specimen Days* is rooted in its *witness*, which derives from the intimacy between the writer and the violence around him, an intimacy that Whitman embraces and observes with an intensity that makes his language vibrate with the awful power of that violence. It achieves its intimacy of address by the writer addressing himself, speaking to himself, musing to himself. Its audience—a mystery.

War: the unseen, the angel of destruction known by Whitman chiefly in terms of its *effects*. Violence manifested in terms of dismemberment, limbs severed from bodies. The dismemberment of the body politic is made manifest in these pages in the dismemberment of the body, in the dismemberment of *bodies*. Yet the bodies themselves are absent—whether dead or alive, they have been transfigured: consigned to a new state, a new state of being. It is the muteness of the limbs that speaks to us; their fragmentation, a testament to the unmaking of the world: "FALMOUTH, VA., *opposite Fredericksburgh, December 21, 1862.*— Begin my visits among the camp hospitals in the army of the Potomac. Spend a good part of the day in a large brick mansion on the banks of the Rappahannock, used as a hospital since the battle—seems to have receiv'd only the worst cases. Out doors, at the foot of a tree, within ten yards of the front of the house, I notice a heap of amputated feet, legs, arms, hands, &c, a full load for a one-horse cart."

"Some of the men were dying. I had nothing to give at that visit, but wrote a few letters to folks home, mothers, &c." All writing for Whitman is a letter, a form of address, a connection made intimate by the writer addressing another, a conveyance at the moment of death (which is the moment of writing)—the moment of life—of the most urgent wishes, strongest emotions, greatest desires, greatest regrets. Writing which would assuage pain, the pain of mortality—even as it gives it *form*. Whitman's writing in *Specimen Days*: amanuensis . . . for those soon-to-be ghosts.

What can writing do for the body in pain? It can render it, give it symbolic presence—but *not* in order to suggest pain's dominion. Rather, to give to Caesar what is Caesar's—but nothing more. Whitman wants to render physical pain, to acknowledge its rule, but more importantly, he wants to render the being of the person in pain in order to give a sense of the person who is resisting its tyranny. Time and again, writing in *Specimen Days* zeros in on this struggle for the reclamation of identity: "A poor fellow in Ward D, with a fearful wound in a fearful condition, was having some loose splinters of bone taken from the neighborhood of the wound. The operation was long, and one of great pain—yet, after it was well commenced, the soldier bore it in silence. He sat up, propp'd— was much wasted—had lain a long time quiet in one position (not for days only but weeks,) a bloodless, brown skinn'd face, with eyes full of determination—belong'd to a New York regiment. There was an unusual cluster of surgeons, medical cadets, nurses, &c., around his bed—I thought the whole thing was done with tenderness, and done well."

What can the body in pain do for *writing*? On the face of it, an irrelevant question. But perhaps there is no greater question for writing for it musters the greatest challenge: the attempt to be adequate to suffering. To not fail in the face of it. To *see* it, to become intimate with it, to come to know the distant journeys behind its bewildered speech—and not sentimentalize it in the translation . . .

Human fate: the same is true of pleasure and writing . . .

Patent-Office Hospital: "go sometimes at night to soothe and relieve particular cases. Two of the immense apartments are fill'd with high and ponderous glass cases, crowded with models in miniature of every kind of utensil, machine or invention, it ever enter'd into the mind of man to conceive; and with curiosities and foreign presents. Between these cases are lateral openings, perhaps eight feet wide and quite deep, and in these were placed the sick, besides a great long double row of them up and down through the middle of the hall. Many of them were very bad cases, wounds and amputations. Then there was a gallery running above the hall in which there were beds also. It was, indeed, a curious scene, especially at night when lit up. The glass cases, the beds, the forms lying there, the gallery above and the marble pavement under foot—the suffering, and the fortitude to bear it in various degrees—occasionally, from some, the groan that could not be repress'd—sometimes a poor fellow dying, with emaciated face and glassy eye, the nurse by his side, the doctor also there, but no friend, no relative—such were the sights but lately in the Patent-office."

The Patent Office houses a vast collection of mechanical contrivances. As such, it is a museum of mechanical invention. How fitting that its marble floors should also house the victims of the first war to utilize mechanical means of mass destruction! They too are on display, as surely as if they were behind glass. Specimens of every new weapon, system, "it ever enter'd into the mind of man to conceive." The Patent-Office Hospital: a grotesque memorial to the a-morality of rationality, and its bloodless patents on death.

Wandering and home: in nineteenth-century America, wandering was possible in a way that assassination, terrorism and mistrust have since made impossible: the relation between the individual and the government— his representatives—was more physically *intimate*. Whitman wanders between the border of battles and make-shift hospitals with an ease and freedom unheard of in the sealed-off, restricted, zoned spacial world of early twentieth-first century America. Whitman could literally *see* more, *witness* more than now would be possible. Seeing and witnessing conflict —especially war or "military action" in the postVietnam era have become things to be licensed, regulated, supervised. With television many more see, but fewer *witness*. Where once witnessing was a way of life, now witness has been professionalized to a few specialized priesthoods. What happens to souls uneducated by witness? Do they become adamantine? Or simply boorish? Witness: for the middle classes now, a dying art but one that may have to be rediscovered . . .

(In the killing zones of the US, internecine violence. Contained and ghettoized. The difficult burden of witness still takes place, but these are lost pockets. The voice of witness rarely breaks out, is rarely heard by those untouched by it, and when it is, the violence of witness is most often co-opted into a melodramatic play—then lost again).

"The White House by Moonlight": *February 24th*—A spell of fine soft weather. I wander about a good deal, sometimes at night under the moon. Tonight took a long look at the President's house. The white portico—the palace-like, tall, round columns, spotless as snow—the walls also—the tender and soft moonlight, flooding the pale marble, and making peculiar faint languishing shades, not shadows—everywhere a soft transparent hazy, thin, blue moon-lace, hanging in the air—the brilliant and extra plentiful clusters of gas, on and around the facade, columns, portico, &c., everything so white, so marbly pure and dazzling, yet soft—the White House of future poems—the gorgeous front, in the trees, under the lustrous flooding moon, full of reality, full of illusion—the forms of the trees, leafless, silent, in trunk and myriad-angles of branches, under the stars and sky—the White House of the land, and of beauty and night—sentries at the gates, and by the portico, silent, pacing there in blue overcoats—stopping you not at all, but eyeing you with sharp eyes, whichever way you move."

Whiteness: innocence. Since this cannot be the case, Whitman's romantic paean to the White House exists as a fantasy, or as fervent wish. Yet it *is* white: the marble reflects back the soft moonlight, creating a ghostly, spectral vision of whiteness that arises out of the surrounding trees. The White House described here is both object and symbol, both reality and fantasy. Whitman's language longs to consecrate it as an emblem of beauty, to find in it an unearthly beauty, a beauty capable of off-setting, even transforming, a republic that is tearing itself to pieces. This may be an illusion, but a necessary one . . . that illusion, then, becomes the necessary reality for the regeneration of the republic.

Whitman: the deliberate artificer of new illusions, new myths (or the refashioner of old ones): "It was a curious sight to see those shadowy columns moving through the night. I stood unobserv'd in the darkness and watch'd them long. The mud was very deep. The men had their usual burdens, overcoats, knapsacks, guns and blankets. Along and along they filed by me, with often a laugh, a song, a cheerful word, but never once a murmur. It may have been odd, but I never before so realized the majesty and reality of the American people *en masse*." For Whitman, the war does not represent pure loss; paradoxically, its brutality is *productive*: it brings out—dramatizes—the "majesty" of the American people. For him the war is not simply internecine struggle or pointless slaughter: the war is the stage upon which the character of the American nation dramatizes itself to itself. Through violence the ideal nation is born. His "blood smutch'd" notebook longs to consecrate the sacrifice of the fallen, the fear and loneliness of the dying, with a purifying national importance. For Whitman, this is as true of the Confederate dead, who gave their life resisting the Union.

All nations require myths built upon illusions: this is a common recognition. Yet illusions account for the surprising durability of nations—and are also their Achilles heel: once the illusions are exhausted, they are done.

"Fortitude as never before . . ." (Pound): "You may hear groans or other sounds of unendurable suffering from two or three of the cots, but in the main there is quiet—almost a painful absence of demonstration; but the pallid face, the dull'd eye, and the moisture on the lip are demonstration enough." Silence in the face of suffering: a sign of the nobility of the cause, the cause of the preservation of the union. To cry out would sully it. Silence is offered as physical sacrifice: an unspoken expression of political solidarity. Whitman accepts the necessity of this silence and suffering, on both sides: they are necessary stages in the achievement of catharsis and the restoration of the body politic. Hence his strange *serenity*.

The mad, wild beauty of war: "But it was the tug of Saturday evening, and through the night and Sunday morning I wanted to make a special note of. It was largely in the woods, and quite a general engagement. The night was very pleasant, at times the moon shining out full and clear, all Nature so calm in itself, the early summer grass so rich, and foliage of the trees—yet there the battle raging, and many good fellows lying helpless, with new accessions to them, and every minute amid the rattle and muskets and the crash of cannon, (for there was artillery contest too,) the red life blood oozing out from heads or trunks or limbs upon that green and dew-cool grass. Patches of the woods take fire, and several of the wounded, unable to move, are consumed—quite large spaces are swept over, burning the dead also—some of the men have their hair and beards singed— some, burns on their faces and hands—others holes burnt in their clothing. The flashes of fire from the cannon, the quick flaring flames and smoke, and the immense roar—the musketry so general, the light nearly bright enough for each side to see the other—the crashing, tramping of men—the yelling—close quarters—we hear the secesh yells—our men cheer loudly back, especially if Hooker is in sight—hand to hand conflicts, each side stands up to it, brave, determin'd as demons, they often charge upon us—a thousand deeds are done worth to write newer greater poems on—and still the woods on fire—still many are not only scorch'd—too many, unable to move, are burn'd to death."

This is not so much Nature (richness, tranquility, life) vs. Man (destruction, violence, death) but Nature's finest drama matched by man's most tragic. Tranquility and ferocity are not simply contrasted, but offered as complimentary dramas, one of silence, one of ferocity, which match one another in the terrible beauty of their realization.

Specimen Days honors Civil War battles such as this as moral spectacle, as the highest form of drama in which the players display their commitment to their drama (the drama of a threatened polity) by consuming themselves on behalf of it. A drama in which the symbolic is made literal.

But it also seeks to register the unnaturalness of this violence: amidst the tranquility of nature, the grotesquerie of war, the scale of it is unrepresentable: "Then the camps of the wounded—O heavens, what scene is this?—is this indeed *humanity*—these butcher's shambles? There are several of them. There they lie, in the largest, in an open space in the woods, from 200 to 300 poor fellows—the groans and screams—the odor of blood, mixed with the fresh scent of the night, the grass, the trees— that slaughter-house! O well is that their mothers, their sisters cannot see them—cannot conceive, and never conceiv'd, these things. One man is shot by a shell, both in the arm and leg—both are amputated—there lie the rejected members. Some have their legs blown off—some bullets through the breast—some indescribably horrid wounds in the face or head, all mutilated, sickening, torn, gouged out—some in the abdomen—some mere boys—many rebels, badly hurt—they take their regular turns with the rest, just the same as any—the surgeons use them just the same. Such is the camp of the wounded—such a fragment, a reflection afar off of the bloody scene—while over all the clear large moon comes out at times softly, quietly shining. Amid the woods, that scene of flitting souls—amid the crack and crash and yelling sounds—the impalpable perfume of the woods—and yet the pungent, stifling smoke—the radiance of the moon, looking from heaven at intervals so placid—the sky so heavenly —the clear-obscure up there, those buoyant upper oceans—a few large placid stars beyond, coming silently and languidly out, and then disappearing— the melancholy, draperied night above, around."

The unthinkable: that this carnage *is* "natural" to us . . .

For Whitman, war is beyond full representation: only snatched, broken fragments, put together in a lyrical helter-skelter idiom, can begin to address its unspeakable violation—and its unspeakeble beauty. Only fragments of the horror can be offered up; anything else is impossible. Again Jabes: "Only in fragments can we read the immeasurable totality."

"To generalize about war is like generalizing about peace. Almost everything is true. Almost nothing is true. At its core, perhaps, war is just another name for death, and yet any soldier will tell you, if he tells the truth, that proximity to death brings with it a corresponding proximity to life. After a fire fight, there is always the immense pleasure of aliveness. The trees are alive. The grass, the soil—everything. All around you things are purely living, and you among them, and the aliveness makes you tremble. You feel an intense, out-of-the-skin awareness of your living self—your truest self, the human being you want to be and then become by the force of wanting it. In the midst of evil, you want to be a good man." (Tim O'Brien, 'How to Tell a True War Story')

"Of scenes like these I say, who writes—whoe'er can write the story? Of many a score—aye, thousands, north and south, of unwrit heroes, unknown heroisms, incredible, impromptu, first-class desperations—who tells? No history ever—no poem sings, no music sounds, those bravest men of all—those deeds. No formal general's report, nor book in the library, nor column in the paper, embalms the bravest, north or south, east or west. Unnamed, unknown, remain and still remain, the bravest soldiers. Our manliest—our boys—our hardy darlings; no picture gives them." Tragedy: the unseen . . . (all history, by definition, is tragic).

How to live *in* tragedy? With "tragic gaiety"?—"Gaiety transfiguring all that dread"? Yeats presupposes an engagement with knowledge, with knowledge of the past as a precondition for "tragic gaiety." But how to live in a nation which, has constructed its identity upon a repression of history—or rewrites it with brazen aplomb as a narrative of innocence? In this world, every moment is invested with edenic freshness and purpose, an innocent forward-reaching that abjures the mess of history, that struggles to rise to live continually in "the ideal."

Who writes, who ever can write the story? The story is that which always escapes the telling. The burden of the writer is to accept this limitation—and continue to write. What is written always carries with it traces of that which did not get written, the story untold. Hence the *necessity* of writing . . .

Whitman's eye always sees war in terms of physical maiming: which for him always borders on sacrilege, as if every body was in itself, an expression of holiness, a tabernacle. By contrast, war is amputation, the severing of limbs, the dismemberment of members belonging to the same body.

Wounding: speech by other means—but speech that cannot be unsaid.

Wounds: openings of flesh, openings into flesh. Forced. Openings into history's nightmares. History inflicted upon the body. The penetration of it. Words undone. The awful mouths. Unspeaking. Spoken for. Gaping and silent in a time without time. Orphans of memory. History's phantasmagoria. Then the desire to become ghostly. The wafer that will not be offered them . . .

Healed wounds contain the potential to spur expression. Unhealed wounds make language more urgent, but more difficult. In the South, an inventive use of language occupies a vital role in its self-identity, yet there is also a plangent, largely subterranean fear—the fear of the vanquished—that language may ultimately be insufficient, ineffective or futile. This is the linguistic legacy of the Civil War. Faulkner: "He did not know that he was dead, then. Sometimes I would lie by him in the dark, hearing the land that was now of my blood and flesh and I would think: Anse. Why Anse. Why are you Anse. I would think about his name until after a while I could see the word as a shape, a vessel, and I would watch him liquify and flow into it like cold molasses flowing out the darkness into the vessel, until the jar stood full and motionless: a significant shape profoundly without life like an empty door frame; and then I would find that I had forgotten the name of the jar. I would think: The shape of my body where I used to be a virgin is in the shape of a   and I couldn't think *Anse* couldn't remember *Anse*. It was not that I could think of myself as no longer unvirgin, because I was three now. And when I would think *Cash* and *Darl* that way until their names would die and solidify into a shape and then fade away, I would say, All right. It doesn't matter. It doesn't matter what they call them" (*As I Lay Dying*).

For Whitman, the war never produced doubt about the ultimate value of language. It was always holy, always a means of consecrating experience.

In war, the mutilation of bodies, both living and dead, embarrasses our self-aggrandizing definitions of ourselves: the italicizing of humanity ("is this indeed *humanity*?") speaks to a wonder at our capacity for self-deception. For Whitman, our capacity for violence transcends language's ability to convey it. Yet the desecrations of war do not, for him, embarrass his notion of the need for the nation to be undivided. That remains sacrosanct.

To peer through catastrophe to make out the shape of a redemptive angel—is this narcissism on a colossal scale—or the first gesture of a necessary utopianism?

If *Specimen Days* is appalled by war, it is also enthralled by it, in love with it, *for* it, at the deepest levels . . . in *Specimen Days*, there is no sense of contradiction at one and the same time in being sickened by its carnage *and* being in love with its pomp and circumstance—and the heroism and valor of its fighting men: "It was a pronouncedly warlike and gay show; the sabres clank'd, the men look'd young and healthy and strong; the electric tramping of so many horses on the hard road, and the gallant bearing, fine seat, and bright faced appearance of a thousand and more handsome young American men, were so good to see." *Specimen Days* offers a new taxonomy of beauty: a taxonomy which values the beauty of the military parade as well as the beauty of death on the battlefield, each category replete with its own aesthetic, its own values, its own ends.

Beauty exists—ironically—in the battlefield tableau of arrested forms: beauty as sacrifice. In its non-ironic form, beauty exists too—but as something beyond us, transcendent, sublime. The purpose of Whitman's writing: to remind us that the fallen world we inhabit, the world of Cain and Abel, is not final; it is only the world we have created. In this sense, the purpose of writing is to convey something that is seen, but also something that is unseen, the "clear-obscure up there," beyond human fashioning, beyond the human genius for destruction. (Language as excess again). The category of the beautiful reminds us of what we are—and of what we are not, of what is, and what is not . . .

Perhaps this is why beauty always has a touch of tragedy about it. Or alternatively, this is why, in its self-sufficiency, in its completion, it can annoy . . .

A frequent pairing in *Specimen Days*: death and beauty. Whenever Whitman references death, he usually finds himself in the presence of beauty. It is as if death provides him with a heightened sense of the beautiful, of the inherent richness of experience which otherwise passes unnoticed, unregarded. The discovered beauty does not compensate for loss, or redeem it; it is just *there*, co-existing in strange familiarity, in strange proximity with the angel of death. Death-in-beauty, beauty- in-death. Death and beauty, beauty and death: an uncanny brethren.

Beauty: the ravishing of the mundane—which is always seen at some *distance*.

To those who are dying, or in pain, beauty must be a phantasm. In Whitman's notebooks, their passing or passage, makes possible the vision of beauty recorded on paper. For Whitman "the beautiful" is paid for in blood, but that sacrifice ennobles, rather than vitiates, it. Whitman's writing is horrified at the effects of battle upon the body, but he never retreats from seeing it as necessary; for him, the Civil War is a "terrible beauty" but one that confirms him in the ultimate justness of the republican cause.

Specimen Days strives to make sacred the *cause*, whatever its sins. In *Specimen Days*, the will-to-redemption is stronger than the will-to-condemnation. Indeed, its sins *are* its catharsis—regeneration through violence, the old curse. In describing a "hell-scene" in which Union forces take revenge for the mutilation of their comrades by Confederate forces, Whitman observes: "Multiply the above by scores, aye hundreds—verify it in all the forms that different circumstances, individuals, places, could afford—light it with every lurid passion, the wolf's, the lion's lapping thirst for blood—the passionate, boiling volcanoes of human revenge for comrades, brothers slain—with the light of burning farms, and heaps of smutting, smouldering black embers—and in the human heart everywhere black, worse embers—and you have an inkling of this war."

In *Specimen Days*, the beauty of the democratic ideals that the Union is struggling to preserve is embodied not only in the stoicism of the suffering soldiers, but in their *physical* beauty. For Whitman, the Civil War is a test of manliness—both the manliness of the Union and that of the Confederacy. The highest form of manliness—beauty—exemplifies the values of the Union. Manliness is expressive of republicanism and republicanism acquires the aura of a heroic, self-less manliness: "*June 18th*—In one of the hospitals I find Thomas Haley, company M, 4th New York cavalry—a regular Irish boy, a fine specimen of youthful physical manliness—shot through the lungs—inevitably dying—came over to this country from Ireland to enlist—has not a single friend or acquaintance here—is sleeping soundly at this moment, (but it is the sleep of death)—has a bullet hole straight through the lung. I saw Tom when first brought here, three days since and didn't suppose he could live twelve hours—(yet he looks well enough in the face to a casual observer.) He lies there with his frame exposed above the waist, all naked, for coolness, a fine built man, the tan not yet bleach'd from his cheeks and neck. It is useless to talk to him, as with his sad hurt, and the stimulants they give him, and the utter strangeness of every object, face, furniture &c., the poor fellow, even when awake, is like some frighten'd, shy animal. Much of the time he sleeps, or half sleeps. (Sometimes I thought he knew more than he show'd.) I often come and sit by him in perfect silence; he will breathe for ten minutes as softly and evenly as a young babe asleep. Poor youth, so handsome, athletic, with profuse beautiful shining hair."

Likewise, Lincoln. March 4, Lincoln's Inauguration: "He was in his plain, two-horse barouche, and look'd very much worn and tired; the lines, indeed, of vast responsibilities, intricate questions, and demands of life and death, cut deeper than ever upon his dark brown face; yet all the old goodness, tenderness, sadness, and canny shrewdness, underneath the old furrows. (I never see that man without feeling that he is one to become personally attach'd to, for his combination of purest, heartiest tenderness, and native western form of manliness."

(But to judge by *Specimen Days* alone, the Civil War had nothing to do with slavery or race. It is curiously full of descriptions of soldiers, but not African Americans. They are invisible, exiled from Whitman's record, from his history).

"*August 12th.*—I see the President almost every day, as I happen to live where he passes to or from his lodgings out of town. He never sleeps at the White House during the hot season, but has quarters at a healthy location some three miles north of the city, the Soldier's home, a United

States military establishment. I saw him this morning about 8 1/2 coming in to business, riding on Vermont avenue, near L street. He always has a company of twenty five or thirty cavalry, with sabres drawn and held upright over their shoulders. They say this guard was against his personal wish, but he let his counselors have their way. The party makes no great show in uniform or horses. Mr. Lincoln on the saddle generally rides a good-sized, easy-going gray horse, is dress'd in plain black, somewhat rusty and dusty, wears a black stiff hat and looks about as ordinary in attire as the commonest man [...] I see very plainly ABRAHAM LINCOLN'S dark brown face, with the deep-cut lines, the eyes always to me with a deep latent sadness in the expression. We have got so that we exchange bows, and very cordial ones [...] They pass'd me once very close, and I saw the President in the face fully, as they were moving slowly, and his look, though abstracted, happen'd to be directed steadily in my eye. He bow'd and smiled, but far beneath his smile I noticed well the expression I have alluded to. None of the artists or pictures has caught the deep, though subtle and indirect expression of this man's face. There is something else there. One of the great portrait painters of two or three centuries ago is needed."

Now we can scarcely conceive of that kind of casual contact. Our sense of *space*, our sense of what a crowd is, of what a city can be—our sense of what a democracy is—has utterly changed. That physical intimacy is now, a relic of nineteenth-century America, perhaps even a relic of ante-bellum Washington. We have now instead the simulacrum of intimacy ... or grotesque parodies of it ...

    1
    There are things
    We live among 'and to see them
    Is to know ourselves':

    Occurrence, a part
    Of an endless series,

    The sad marvels;

Of this was told
A tale of our wickedness.
It is not our wickedness [. . .]
        —George Oppen, *Of Being Numerous*

Of Stewart. C. Glover, 20 years old, company E, 5th Wisconsin in a Washington hospital: "He kept a diary, like so many of the soldiers. On the day of his death he wrote the following lines in it, *to-day the doctor says I must die—all is over with me—ah, so young to die.* On another blank leaf he pencill'd to his brother, *dear brother Thomas, I have been brave but wicked—pray for me.*

"It is not our wickedness" [. . .]

But what it is cannot be spoken . . .

Whitman's writing reports to the reader the words of the dying and those of the dead. Through his "blood smutch'd" notebooks, it is possible to sense the dimensions of the unsaid, the dimensions of the catastrophe that was the Civil War. Through them, Glover's last scratched-out, hospital-ward words sound into the twenty first century. Whitman's book constitutes itself as a letter to the world. It acknowledges the signal importance of self-expression, but equally the importance of being *heard.* The greatest pain: speaking into the darkness, unaccompanied, unheard. *Specimen Days* works to constitute the American reading public as an audience for the many anonymous private and difficult passings-away in the battlefield shambles and hospitals during the Civil War. It longs to perform the death-bed vigil witness to and for the nation that Whitman performed in his self-chosen ministry as comfort-giver to the wounded and dying . . .

"*Frank H. Irwin, company E, 93d Pennsylvania—died May I, '65—My letter to his mother.*—Dear Madam: No doubt you and Frank's friends have heard the sad fact of his death in hospital here, through his uncle, or the lady from Baltimore, who took his things. (I have not seen them, only heard of them visiting Frank.) I will write you a few lines—as a casual friend that sat by his death-bed. Your son, corporal Frank H. Irwin, was wounded near Fort Fisher, Virginia, March 25th, 1865—the wound was in the left knee, pretty bad. He was sent up to Washington, was receiv'd in ward C, Armory-square hospital, March 28th—the wound became worse, and on the 4th of April the leg was amputated a little above the knee—the operation was perform'd by Dr. Bliss, one of the best surgeons in the army—he did the whole operation himself—there was a good deal of bad matter gather'd—the bullet was found in the knee. For a couple of weeks afterwards he was doing pretty well. I visited and sat by him frequently, as he was fond of having me. The last ten or twelve days of April I saw that his case was critical. He previously had some fever, with cold spells. The last week in April he was much of the time flighty—but always mild and gentle. He died first of May. The actual cause of death was paemia (the absorption of the matter in the system instead of its discharge.) Frank, as far as I saw, had everything requisite in surgical treatment, nursing, etc. He had watches much of the time. He was so good, well-behaved and affectionate, I myself liked him very much. I was in the habit of coming in afternoons and sitting by him, and soothing him, and he liked to have me—liked to put his arm out and lay his hand upon my knee—would keep it so a long while. Toward the last he was more restless and flighty at night—often he fancied himself with his regiment—by his talk sometimes seem'd as if his feelings were hurt by being blamed by his officers for something he was entirely innocent of—said, "I never in my life was thought capable of such a thing, and never was." At other times he would fancy himself talking as it seem'd to children or such like, his relatives I suppose, and giving them good advice; would talk to them a long while. All the time he was out of his head not one single bad word or idea escaped him. It was remark'd that many a man's conversation in his senses was not half as good as Frank's delirium. He seem'd quite willing to die—he had become very weak and had suffer'd a good deal, and was perfectly resign'd, poor boy. I do not know his past life, but I feel as if it must have been good. At any rate, what I saw of him here, under the most trying circumstances, with a painful wound, and among strangers, I can say that he behaved so brave, so composed, and so sweet and affectionate, it could not have been surpass'd. And now like many other noble and good men, after serving his country as a soldier, he has yielded up his young life at the very outset in her service. Such things are gloomy—yet there is a text, "God doeth all things well"—the meaning of which, after due time, appears to the soul.

I thought perhaps a few words, though from a stranger, about your son, from one who was with him at the last, might be worth while— for I loved the young man, though I but saw him immediately to lose him. I am merely a friend visiting the hospitals occasionally to cheer the wounded and the sick.   W. W."

The achievement of *Specimen Days*: Whitman allowed the body in pain to *speak*, to express its deepest fears and pains, countering the institutional expectation that the dying body die isolated and in silence. Offering the consolation of presence—symbolically, human solidarity— in an environment in which the dying body exists as a reproach to the medical profession: this was Whitman's most radical *act*—an act of radical intimacy.

". . . we are, however, only *ourselves*, from the point within us where the other, the mortal other, resonantes" (Derrida).

But a self—a being in flux—always dependent *upon* the other. To the Civil War, to Irwin—and men like him—Whitman owes the greatest debt: his self, his identity as a writer, his *world*.

Is not the diary an expression of the hope that one person's experience— world—will not be totally lost to oblivion? And yet is not its value equally the value it offers the individual in providing an opportunity to crystallize the most urgent observations and emotions of the day on the page? Every diary is thus the expression of authorship and the rejection of it.

Specimen Days is a text in which irony is notably absent, except for the over-riding ironies inherent in the war itself. So Whitman's writing, his observations of what he saw and heard and felt, is ironic without being overtly so. War: the supreme ironist—and the real author of this text.

In Whitman's notebook, Washington is a city of refugees, refugees from the war, the wounded and sick and its deserters: "Almost every day I see squads of them, sometimes two or three at a time, with a small guard; sometimes ten or twelve, under a larger one. (I hear that desertions from the army now in the field have often averaged 10000 a month.

One of the commonest sights in Washington is a squad of deserters.)" A war famous for its sacrifice and violence is also a war in which tens of thousands turned their backs on sacrifice-to-cause. What then of heroism? Cowardice? Sacrifice? What the Civil War *was*? Deserters: bearers of social stigma because their action challenges the Manichean mythology of war, which allows for only one side to be good, only one side to be bad—a mythology necessary to the prosecution of war.

In American popular mythology, Civil War deserters do not exist. It is as if they all returned unnoticed, melted back into the rank and file, charged and died heroic deaths on the battlefield.

"The hospital part of the drama from '61 to '65 deserves indeed to be recorded. O that many-threaded drama, with its sudden and strange surprises, its confounding of prophecies, its moments of despair, the dread of foreign interference, the interminable campaigns, the bloody battles, the mighty and cumbrous and green armies, the drafts and bounties—the immense money expenditure, like a heavy-pouring constant rain—with, over the whole land, the last three years of the struggle, an unending, universal mourning-wail of women, parents, orphans—the marrow of the tragedy concentrated in those Army Hospitals—(it seem'd sometimes as if the whole interest of the land, North and South, was one vast central hospital, and all the rest of the affair but flanges)—those forming the untold and unwritten history of the war—infinitely greater (like life's) than the the few scraps and distortions that are ever told or written." *Specimen Days*: the first history of a war to be written from the point of view of the body in war—the wounded, the sick and the dying. This "untold and unwritten history of the war" tells more about the physical experience of being in war—more about the fate of the body in war— than anything else. A history of the mutilation, sickness and death of the body outside—and in—the "one vast central hospital" of the nation.

September, 1862: A Letter from Maj. William Child to His Wife, after Antietam:

"My Dear Wife:

It is now evening. I am very much better than I have been, but am yet as yellow as an orange. There is nothing of interest here to write unless I give you some of our hospital operations. How many patients we have I do not know—probably four hundred and fifty certain. The wounds in all parts you can think, but seven tenths of all have suffered amputation. Many die each day. Some are doing well. No one can begin to estimate the amount of agony after a great battle. We win a great victory. It goes through the country. The masses rejoice, but if all could see the thousands of poor suffering dieing men their rejoicing would turn to weeping. For days our wounded after the last great battle lay in and about old barns and in the yards on straw. It was impossible to take care of them all for three or four days—and were not removed from the barns for three weeks. Now many will recover to live a poor maimed old soldier—while others are fast going to the grave.

When I think of the battle of Antietam it seems so strange. Who permits it? To see or feel that a power is in existence that can and will hurl masses of men against each other in deadly conflict—slaying each other by the thousands—mangling and deforming their fellow men is almost impossible. But it is so and why we can not know . . ."

The most famous line of *Specimen Days*: "The real war will never get in the books." Again and again, the dilemma in American letters of not being *heard*. The fate of American writers: they write expecting silence; they write with the expectation that the nation will not receive their writing, that they will not be *heard*. Writing in, out of and to silence: it turns literature on itself, forces it to *do* for itself. At the same time, this exile from community enables experimentation, risk-taking, invention; but it exacts a terrible price for its "freedom."

The pathetic fallacy? In the last stages of the war, nature is no longer figured as a bystander but is seen as an active respondent to its calamities: "There, since this war, and the wide and deep national agitation, strange analogies, different combinations, a different sunlight or absence of it; different products even out of the ground. After every great battle, a great storm. Even civic events the same. On Saturday last, a forenoon like whirling demons, dark, with slanting rain, full of rage; and the afternoon, so calm, so bathed with flooding splendor from heaven's most excellent sun, with atmosphere of sweetness; so clear, it show'd the stars, long, long before they were due." More important than the fallacy is the recognition that nature and culture are not separate, but interdependent and mutually conditioning and that the consequences of human action ripple out in a multitude of unforeseeable ways.

To bring to mind the mutilated bodies of the war, to make the sovereign rule of pain intrude into more removed worlds, politer realms, the future, even—this is the *work* Whitman's notebooks long to do. The Civil War passages in *Specimen Days* desire to transgress borders—the border between the disfiguring world of war and the muffled world of civilian decorum, the border between official Washington and its teeming street life, the border between the socially acceptable and the socially unacceptable, even the border between present and future. It longs to create an environment in which (some of) the fractured realities of war-time America could, at least momentarily, be brought together, and experienced in all their unlived relatedness: "Inauguration Ball. *March 6.*—I have been up to look at the dance and supper-rooms, for the inauguration ball at the Patent Office; and I could not help thinking, what a different scene they presented to my view a while since, fill'd with a crowded mass of the worst wounded of the war, brought in from second Bull Run, Antietam, and Fredricksburgh. To-night, beautiful women, perfumes, the violin's sweetness, the polka and the waltz; then the amputation, the blue face, the groan, the glassy eye of the dying, the clotted rag, the odor of wounds and blood, and many a mother's son amid strangers passing away untended there, (for the crowd of the badly hurt was great, and much for nurse to do, and much for surgeon."

Unionism through martyrdom: "*April 16, '65.*—I find in my notes of the time, this passage on the death of Abraham Lincoln: He leaves for America's history and biography, so far, not only its most dramatic reminiscence—he leaves, in my opinion, the greatest, best, most characteristic, artistic, moral personality. Not that he had faults and show'd them in the Presidency; but honesty, goodness, shrewdness, conscience, and (a new virtue, unknown to other lands, an hardly yet really known here, but the foundation and tie of all, as the future will grandly develop,) UNIONISM, in its truest and amplest sense, form'd the hard-pan of his character. These he seal'd with his life. The tragic splendour of his death, purging, illuminating all, throws round his form, his head, an aurole that will remain and grow brighter through time, while history lives, and love of country lasts. By many has this Union been help'd; but if one name, one man, must be pick'd out, he, most of all, is the conservator of it, to the future. He was assassinated—but the Union is not assassinated—*ça ira*! One falls and another falls. The soldier drops, sinks like a wave—but the ranks of the ocean eternally press on. Death does its work, obliterates a hundred, a thousand—President, general, captain, private—but the Nation is immortal."

July 10, 2002. This morning it has been raining hard. Great gusts & sheets of rain falling slantwise from the heavens; the rain sluices down my window panes in watery streams, making the glass and the world outside it blurry & indistinct. Today makes it one hundred and thirty seven years on from Whitman's elegiac entry on Lincoln. Since then the Spanish-American War, World War I, World War II, the Korean War, the Vietnam War, The Persian Gulf War ("Desert Storm") and now, "The War on Terrorism." Not to speak of the myriad "campaigns," "interventions," and all the forms of "assistance" that escape popular memory. Are we the future of Whitman's illusion?

American fear I: What if the Union can live *only* in writing, symbolically?

American fear II: What if the Union continues to live, to thrive, but—without the possibility for actual dissent, or change?

American fear III: What happens to a nation that can't even remember its own great illusions?

And yet history has often been the story of illusions that "suddenly" metamorphose into reality: that is the hope, as well as the fear.

An American invention: "The releas'd prisoners of war are now coming up from the southern prisons. I have seen a number of them. The sight is worse than any sight of battle-fields, or any collection of wounded, even the bloodiest. There was, (as a sample) one large boat load, of several hundreds, brought about the 25th, to Annapolis; and out of that whole number only three individuals were able to walk from the boat. The rest were carried ashore and laid down in one place or another. Can those be *men*—those little livid brown, ash-streak'd, monkey-looking dwarfs?—are they really not mummied, dwindled corpses? They lay there, most of them, quite still, but with a horrible look in their eyes and skinny lips (often with not enough flesh on the lips to cover their teeth.) Probably no more appalling sight was ever seen on this earth. (There are deeds, crimes, that may be forgiven; but this is not among them. It steeps its perpetrators in blackest, escapeless, endless damnation. Over 50,000 have been compell'd to die the death of starvation; reader, did you ever try to realize what *starvation* really is?—in those prisons—and in the land of plenty.) An almost indescribable meanness, tyranny, aggravating course of insults, almost incredible—was evidently the rule of treatment through all the southern military prisons. The dead there are not to be pitied as much as some of the living that come from there—if they can be call'd living—many of them are mentally imbecile, and will never recuperate." The first modern war invented the first concentration camps as we know them— an *American* invention. A catastrophe of morality— of precedent—from which one wonders if there can be a return. A catastrophe of suffering: if the purpose of war is injurying, if war is a process of "reciprocal injurying," (Scarry) the Southern prisons invented a new role for themselves as an extension of the war: not a cessation of its aggressions, but an intensification of them. War unbounded—and the ruins of the dream of the Enlightenment in its wake. The more obvious legacy: Dachau, Bergen-Belsen, Dresden, Hiroshima and Nagasaki. The less obvious legacy: suffering in excess of tactical need; no longer will a calculus of the *sufficiency* of suffering constrain military action. Power unembarrassed by the transgression of morality. Power finally *freed* to be itself . . .

Catastrophe requires a new language, a new logic of being-in-the-world, but not a forgetting of the old language, the old being. A new "intertextuality" then which rejects the sovereignty of self, the legitimated disenfranchisement of the other—impossible, but necessary nonetheless. (Literature as its failed—but still flickering— approximation).

The least a witness of disaster, a witness to an epoch of deliberately-inflicted, extreme suffering, can do is *not* say "At least I am not guilty of that."

"At intervals all day long sounded out the wild music of those peculiar army cries. They would be commenc'd by one regiment or brigade, immediately taken up by others, and at length whole corps and armies would join in these wild triumphant choruses. It was one of the characteristic expressions of the western troops, and became a habit, serving as a relief and an outlet to the men— a vent for their feelings of victory, returning peace, &c. Morning, noon, and afternoon, spontaneous, for occasion or without occasion, these huge, strange cries differing from any other, echoing through the open air for many a mile, expressing youth, joy, wildness, irrepressible strength, and the ideas of advance and conquest, sounded along the swamps and uplands of the South, floating to the skies [. . .] This exuberance continued until the armies arrived at Raleigh. There the news of the President's murder was receiv'd. Then no more shouts or yells, for a week. All the marching was comparatively muffled. It was very significant—hardly a loud word or laugh in many of the regiments. A hush and silence pervaded all." Silence: acknowledgement of the sovereignty of necessity. And the chastisement of hope, in a wordless rhetoric.

And always the need to *interpret* silence, to say what it means. As if it would overwhelm language if left unaccompanied; which is to say, the terror of an unchangeable reality, remorselessly expansive, utterly intransigent . . .

Whitman's uneasy vigil: towards silence, *Specimen Days* displays the utmost reverence, the deepest fear.

Hence the use of the fragment form—which is both saying and not saying.

Whitman's final calculus: "The dead in this war—there they lie strewing the fields and woods and valleys and battle-fields of the south— Virginia, the Peninsula—Malvern Hill and Fair Oaks—the banks of the Chickahominy—the terraces of Fredericksburg—Antietam bridge— the gristly ravines of the Manassas—the bloody promenade of the

Wilderness—the varieties of the *strayed* dead, (the estimate of the War department is 25,000 national soldiers kill'd in battle and never buried at all, 5,000 drown'd—15,000 inhumed by strangers, or on the march in haste, in hitherto unfound localities—2,000 graves cover'd by sand and mud by Mississippi freshets, 3,000 carried away by caving-in of banks, &c.,) —Gettysburg, the West, Southwest—Vicksburgh, Chattanooga— the trenches of Petersburgh—the numberless battles, camps, hospitals everywhere—the crop reap'd by the mighty reapers, typhoid, dysentery, inflammations—the blackest and loathesomest of all, the dead and living burial pits, the prison pens of Andersonville, Salisbury, Belle-Isle, &c., (not Dante's pictured hell and all its woes, its degradations, filthy torments, excell'd those prisons)—the dead, the dead, the dead, *our* dead—or South or North, ours all, (all, all, all finally dear to me)—or East or West— Atlantic coast or Mississippi valley—somewhere they crawl'd to die, alone, in bushes, low gullies or on the sides of hills—(there in secluded spots their skeletons, bleach'd bones, tufts of hair, buttons, fragments of clothing, are occasionally found yet)—our young men once so handsome and so joyous, taken from us—the son from the mother, the husband from the wife, the dear friend from the dear friend—the clusters of camp graves, in Georgia, the Carolinas, and in Tennessee—the single graves left in the woods or by the road-side, (hundreds, thousands, obliterated)—the corpses floated down the rivers, and caught and lodged (dozens, scores, floated down the upper Potomac, after the cavalry engagements, the pursuit of Lee, following Gettysburg)—some lie at the bottom of the sea—the general million, and the special cemeteries in all the States—the infinite dead—the land entire saturated" perfumed with their impalpable ashes' exhalation in Nature's chemistry distill'd, and shall be so forever, in every future grain of wheat and ear of corn, and every flower that grows, and every breath we draw)—not only Northern dead leavening Southern soil—thousands, aye tens of thousands, of Southerners, crumble to-day in Northern earth."

Specimen Days: ghost writing for the million dead. Yet they are not lost; their dust intermingles with the earth's, becoming part of it, part of nature, part of its regenerative beauty, part of us. Bloodletting as sacred communion: the desire is to see the violence of war as ushering in a new era in the human relation to nature. For Whitman, honoring nature then becomes synonymous with honoring the dead.

Ghost writing: the writing of memory. The long handwritten script that flows down the page, moving from one page to the next. The script that does not get written—that is unwritable. The unwritten script between the lines, "in" the white spaces that separate the words, that separate the lines. Memory: the incessant *re-imagination* of the dead, their ghosts, what they said, or might have said . . . the ghostly handwriting the living must decipher . . .

Sorties: *Specimen Days'* last, lengthy set of finely-observed meditations upon the changing face of nature are not only a retreat to a more exquisite and salubrious environment removed from the death wards of the war; they are a way of connecting with the legions of the dead. Nature—or the *writing* of nature— is to restore Whitman's "one vast central hospital of the nation": "Who knows, (I have it in my fancy, my ambition,) but the pages now ensuing may carry ray of sun, or smell of grass or corn, or call of bird, or gleam of stars by night, or snow flakes falling fresh and mystic, to denizen of heated city house, or tired workman or workingwoman?—or may be in sick room or prison—to serve as a cooling breeze, or Nature's aroma, to some fever'd mouth or latent pulse."

In its *moment*, the writing of nature, nature on paper, makes everything possible. That is its beauty—and its tragedy: *August 25, [1878] 9–10 a.m.*—I sit by the edge of the pond, everything quiet, the broad polish'd surface spread before me—the blue of the heavens and the white clouds reflected from it—and flitting across, now and then, the reflection of some flying bird. Last night I was down here with a friend till after midnight; everything a miracle of splendor—the glory of the stars, and the completely rounded moon—the passing clouds, silver and luminous-tawny—now and then masses of vapory illuminated scud—and silently by my side my dear friend. The shades of the trees, and patches of moonlight on the grass—the softly blowing breeze, and just-palpable odor of the neighboring ripening corn—the indolent and spiritual night, inexpressibly rich, tender, suggestive—something to altogether to filer through one's soul, and nourish and feed and soothe the memory long afterwards."

Chapter 4
The Treason of an Accent:
Emily Dickinson's *Letters*

"A chronicler who recites events without distinguishing between major and minor ones acts in accordance with the following truth: nothing that has ever happened should be regarded as lost for history. To be sure, only a redeemed mankind receives the fullness of its past—which is to say, only for a redeemed mankind has its past become citable in all its moments. Each moment it has lived becomes a citation *à l'ordre du jour*—and that day is Judgment Day."
—Walter Benjamin, "Theses on the Philosophy of History"

Forging a new language in a world suspicious of heresy: how to live in, live with, a community of believers and not believe? Or not believe as it does? How to forge a relationship in writing with that which lies beyond—as well as with the strange territories within? How to forge a new self—new selves—in a world distrustful of self-fashioning? Forging a new language accented by heresy: Dickinson's poetry inhabits the chastened form of the hymn, but wills a wildness of language, a linguistic wilderness, into being. This is true, too, of her letters, which avail of the open space of the page, see the open space of the page as the field of the unsayable, the field of the unknowable, of the necessary-to-say . . .

In Dickinson's writing, there is not the demonization of the wilderness (of nature, of writing) manifest in Puritan writing, but an openness to it, a serenity before its godlessness, a serenity before its *godliness*. Dickinson's poetry and letters produce a wilderness of words within which there are only ghost-like paths. Stratagems of the dissident: allegory, riddle, gnomic utterance, compression, elision, entire *scales* of ambiguity . . .

Dickinson's writing: treasonous in its independence, treasonous in its commitment to that which is not self-evident—enigma—and treasonous in its commitment to ecstasy:

The Treason of an accent
Might Ecstasy transfer

Of her effacing Fathom
Is no Recovery—
[No. 450, 1876—to T.W. Higginson]

Passion as an affront—a treasonous—practice: "You think me "uncontrolled"—I have no Tribunal." [No. 265, 1862—to T.W. Higginson]. Or as Susan Howe puts it: "Splendor is subversive to the Collective will" (*My Emily Dickinson*).

Dickinson's letters: a script intent upon making connections with the other (the self) as well as with the living and the dead; they are a reaching out (and a withholding), an expression of the desire to be in dialogue with the world (as well as "the self"), an expression of the need to be in dialogue with desire (as well as loss). Each letter is made up of other letters, fragments from other texts, echoes from other texts—always the resonance of another *body*. Each letter is a composition born out of the greeting it makes to the world, and the world of letters "behind" it. And each of Dickinson's letters translates that written legacy anew.

Her letters employ a language that make possible a certain kind of being, one that is outside the "Collective Will" but in communication with it: "I thought I would write again. I write you many letters with pens which are not seen. Do you receive them?" [No. 175, 1854—to Dr. and Mrs. J.G. Holland]

Letters as transforming, powerful, dangerous:—"What a Hazard a Letter is"! [No. 1007, 1885—to T.W. Higginson]. Dangerous because of their power to unsettle all that appears fixed, permanent, settled, all the more because they take place in an arena of intimate address. Writing: the formula of the real.

Most letters traduce the world by domesticating it, robbing it of its wonder. Dickinson's letters do not make the world less strange; rather, they create a medium through which the original strangeness of the world becomes evident: "Susie—it is a little thing to say how lone it is—anyone can do it, but to wear the loneness next your heart for weeks, when you sleep, and when you wake, ever missing something, *this*, all cannot say, and it baffles me. I would paint a portrait which would bring the tears, had I canvass for it, and the scene should be—*solitude*, and the figures—solitude—and the lights and shades, each a solitude. I could fill a chamber with landscapes so lone, men should pause and weep there; then haste grateful home, for a loved one left. Today has been a fair day, very still and blue. Tonight, the crimson children are playing in the West, and tomorrow will be colder. In all I number you. I want to think of you each hour in the day. What are you saying—doing—I want to walk with you, as seeing yet unseen." [No. 176, 1854—to Susan Gilbert (Dickinson)].

Seeing the world afresh, anew, in its original wonder, *in itself* stands as an act of defiance against settled orthodoxies, calcified traditions, habituated ways of being. Dickinson's writing: a record of revolutionary seeing, ceaselessly revising itself.

The lure of the outsider, the outcast (no American literature without it): "Where do you think I've strayed, and from what new errand returned? I have come from "*to* and *fro*, and walking up, and down" the same place that Satan hailed from, when God asked him where he'd been, but not to illustrate further I tell you I have been dreaming, dreaming a *golden* dream, with eyes all the while wide open, and I guess it's almost morning, and besides I have been at work, providing the "food that perisheth," scaring the timorous dust, and being obedient and kind. *I* call it kind obedience in the books the Shadows write in, it may have another name." [No. 37—1850, to Abiah Root]

American culture: a dream-work in which writers are cast as Satanic progeny (or else are ignored as hapless innocents).

American myth idolizes the outcast, as well as the outsider, but in actuality, those who menace American goodness are demonized or exiled. Only a nation with an intense distrust of the threat posed by outsiders, by outsideness, would need to perform over and again, obsessively, the value of the outsider, the value of its own receptivity to difference.

Hence our mania to homogenize the world, to purge or assimilate "outsideness," to render everything benign in a kingdom of sameness. By its mere mode of address, its fineness of distinctions, Dickinson's writing defies this "imperial affliction"; it is too aware of the "internal difference, /Where the Meanings, are" (No. 258).

American fate: freedom signified only by heresy . . . in that environment, freedom —and its death—is as palpable as darkness.

A new Calvary: The transformation of the sacred—the religion of a tortured, unearthly god of love who dies for an unregenerate humanity— into something else, not secular but idiosyncratically sacred—a sacredness based upon a rewriting, a re-inflection, a reworking of New England Puritanism. The transubstantiation of Christian language and iconography in Dickinson yields a new worshipfulness—and a new object of worship: writing as sacred ritual, as transgression, as spiritual performance, as erotic enactment; writing as a way of reverencing whatever the world may *at that moment* become: "Thank the dear little snow flakes, because they fall *today* rather than some vain *weekday*, when the world and the cares of the world try so hard to keep me from my departed friend—and thank you, too, dear Susie, that you never weary of me, or never *tell* me so, and that when the world is cold, and the storm sighs e'er so piteously, I am sure of one sweet shelter, one covert from the storm! The bells are ringing, Susie, north, and east, and south, and *your own* village bell, and the people who love God, are expecting to go to the meeting; dont *you* go Susie, not to *their* meeting, but come with me this morning to the church within our hearts, where the bells are always ringing, and the preacher whose name is Love—shall intercede there for us!" [No. 77—1852, to Susan Gilbert (Dickinson)].

And writing as doubt; the rich, swooning language of despairing affirmation that works out her new Calvary: "Oh my darling one, how long you wander from me, how weary I grow of waiting and looking, and calling for you; sometimes I shut my eyes, and shut my heart towards you, and try hard to forget you because you grieve me so, but you'll never go away, Oh you never will—say, Susie, promise me again, and I will smile faintly—and take up my little cross again of sad—*sad* separation. How vain it seems to *write*, when one knows how to feel—how much more near and dear to sit beside you, talk with you, hear the tones of your

voice; so hard to "deny thyself, and take up thy cross, and follow me"—
give me strength, Susie, write me of hope and love, and of hearts that
endured, and great was their reward of "Our Father who in Heaven." [. . .]
Never be mournful, Susie—be happy and have cheer, for how many of
the long days have gone away since I wrote you—and it is almost noon,
and soon the night will come, and then there is one less day of the long
pilgrimage." [No. 73—1852, to Susan Gilbert (Dickinson)]

Writing: for Dickinson, the attempt to recreate in language an intimacy
that is *elsewhere*.

*And is this not the signature of much American literature—against the emptiness
of American space, the attempt to use the written page, the book, to create a
community of sympathy, however imaginary?*

The Letters: one long apostrophe to death, but they work out an erotics
of death in which morbidity figures as a form of pleasure, like writing . . .

Is there a national literature more ghostly? More violent—and more
haunted? (Hence the Gothic—a genre suitable to a fallen nation, but
one which can acknowledge its fallenness only allegorically). In her
hauntedness, Dickinson shows a quintessentially American soul.

The scene of Dickinson's writing: a circling back, a returning, to the
question of fulfillment. Dickinson's poetry dazzles with its ability to
evoke uncanny states of being, uncanny paradises—even if they ultimately
remain largely out of sight. A form of writing that prefigures or enacts
or defers paradise (all at once). The immanence of death intensifies and
threatens the writing of paradise. Dickinson at nineteen: "Tis strange
that a promise lives, and brightens, when the day that fashioned it, has
mouldered, & stranger still, a promise looking to the day of Valentines for
its fulfillment." [No. 27, 1849—to William Cowper Dickinson] In May
of 1866, at fifty-six, Dickinson's last known letter:

> Little Cousins
> Called back.
> Emily.

Death as solitude, death as repose, as fulfillment, or promise of fulfillment—
how many of Dickinson's sentences drive toward that ending? The myth
of the recluse obscures a more important withdrawal: the withdrawal not
so much of the writer, but of her *work*. Solitude as necessity—and tactic.
The solitude of the work (Blanchot). Solitude, not isolation. A solitude that
finds withdrawal to be the most complete means of reporting upon the
world as it is *apprehended*: "[. . .] yet the "Infinite Beauty"—of which you
speak comes too near to seek" [No. 319, 1866—to T. W. Higginson]

Death: for Dickinson, the great Preceptor. Not life but death. Or life-
as-death. Life is an "apparitional pleasure" [No. 316, 1866—to T. W.
Higginson] made possible by the presence-in-absence that is language . . .
one absence *invoking* the other . . .

The body: also "apparitional pleasure."

Paradise: Dickinson's writing strains to see it—to apprehend it—however
fleetingly, in the here and now: "Bless God that we catch faint glimpses
of his brighter Paradise from *occasional* Heaven *here*!" [No. 107, 1853—to
Susan Gilbert (Dickinson)]. This is not an outright disavowal of God;
rather, He becomes recreated by her, and paradise becomes a state of
being not simply reserved for the afterlife, but a state of being in which
an ecstatic communion of souls is made possible through an ecstatic
language. Through this invocation— inflected with passion, longing and
power—absence is transubstantiated into presence, loss into gain—or the
promise of it: "Forgive me if I prize the Grace—superior to the Sign."
[No. 277, 1862—to Samuel Bowles]

The scene of Dickinson's writing: American literary exile before the
modernist invention of literary exile: "To escape enchantment, one must
always flee." [No. 319, 1866—to T. W. Higginson]. But like all great exilic
consciousnesses, Dickinson's remains fastened upon what it has separated
itself *from*—as well as attending—with uncanny intensity—to the world
to come; to the worlds that are at every instant in process of becoming . . .

The wonders of the visible world, no less than those of the invisible . . .
"You say it is hot and dry. It is very dry here, tho' now for two or three

days the air is fine and cool—Everything is so beautiful, it's a real Eden here; how happy we shall be roaming round it together! The trees are getting over the effect of the Canker worm, and we hope we may have some apples yet, tho' we cant tell now—but we feel very thankful that the leaves are not all gone, and there's a few green things which hav'nt been carried away—" [No. 131, 1853—to Austin Dickinson]

The death of the supernatural: "I was thinking, today, as I noticed, that the "Supernatural," was only the Natural, disclosed." [No. 280, 1863—to T.W. Higginson]

Dickinson's Thanatos: "Life is death we're lengthy at, death the hinge to life." [No. 281, 1863—to Louise and Frances Norcross]

In Puritan writing, the world is a sign: it needs to be deciphered in order to understand God's purpose. In Dickinson's writing, the language she uses to invoke it, requires deciphering. Again, the sovereign ghost of American writing.

For Dickinson, poetry is also a kind of prayer, but prayer without an altar or unalloyed fealty to the Christian divine. How to *have*, be in, two worlds, two kingdoms? The double-consciousness of the would-be believer: the opportunity and the predicament of Dickinson's writing. "But I feel that I have not yet made my peace with God. I am still a s[tran]ger—to the delightful emotions which fill your heart. I have perfect confidence in God & his promises & yet know not why, I feel the world holds a predominant place in my affections. I do not feel that I could give up all for Christ, were I called to die. Pray for me Dear A. that I may yet enter into the kingdom, that there may be room left for me in the shining courts above." [No. 13, 1846—to Abiah Root]. Dickinson's consciousness is, then, deeply historical, but one held in thrall by a passionate, but undeceived, utopianism.

Historical consciousness I: "The Pilgrim's Empire seems to stoop—I hope it will not fall— [No. 721, 1881—to Mrs. J.G. Holland]

Historical consciousness II: "The past is not a package one can lay away." [No. 830, 1883—to Maria Whitney]

Historical consciousness III: "But the world is sleeping in ignorance and error, sir, and we must be crowing cocks, and singing larks, and a rising sun to awake her; or else we'll pull society up to the roots, and plant it in a different place. We'll build Alms-houses, and transcendental State prisons, and scaffolds—we will blow out the sun, and the moon, and encourage invention. Alpha shall kiss Omega—we will ride up the hill of glory—Hallelujah, all hail!" [No. 34, 1850—to George H. Gould] A ludic language—but one that mocks the presumption behind correction. In it, too, the awareness of the paradoxes and limitations of revolutionary action, of revolutionary writing which would usher in a new world: "We'll build Alms-houses, and transcendental State prisons, and scaffolds." Remaking the world in the image of a utopian dream may be emancipatory, but also not: it —inevitably—repeats the mistakes of the past. Dickinson was never simply beguiled by her own revolution in style and form: her writing always announces its own power— and its limitations.

Pain: the master emotion in Dickinson's writing. The starkness and purity of her *openness* to it (The willingness to give herself over to it. Submission to it as the price of intimacy. "May I change places, Austin? *I* dont care how sharp the pain is, not if it dart like arrows, or pierce bone and bone like the envenomed barb, I should be twice, *thrice* happy to bear it in your place." [No. 66, 1851—to Austin Dickinson]. Through pain comes knowledge of dispossession, knowledge of the pain and isolation of the dispossessed. Withdrawal: the strategy by which worldly pain can be gradually explored, entered into, as a determined explorer embarks upon the exploration of a forbidding new continent . . .

The body as text: "open me carefully" [No. 94, 1852—to Susan Gilbert (Dickinson)]. In Dickinson's writing, the body is not explicitly referenced; at most, there are only synecdoches for it. Through an intense act of the will, the body is translated into abstraction, pure textuality— but a textuality that is everywhere shaped and possessed by the absent "language" of the body . . .

The proximity of pain and ecstasy in Dickinson's writing: each bleeds into the other. Pain: the portal of ecstasy; if nothing else, it takes one beyond the self, beyond its complacent fictions of totality. Writing: A struggle, but a blissful one, indeed a blessed one: "'Audacity of Bliss, said Jacob to the Angel "I will not let thee go except I bless thee—"' [No.1042, 1886—ED's last letter to T.W Higginson]

The exquisite attention to pain in Dickinson enables the finest apprehension of the strains in social existence; no nuance of relationship escapes detection. Though little in her writing commends itself to us as overtly social, "the social" registers itself in part as the pain of relationship.

Home: for Dickinson, a utopian space which, despite its shortcomings, is *made* to symbolize a redemptive social life based upon mutuality (but a mutuality based upon a nineteenth-century world of domestic assistance): "Home is a holy thing—nothing of doubt or distrust can enter its blessed portals. I feel it more and more as the great world goes on, and one and another forsake, in whom you place your trust—here seems indeed to be a bit of Eden, which not the sin of *any* can utterly destroy—smaller it is indeed, and it may be less fair, but fairer and *brighter* than all the world beside." [No. 59, 1851—to Austin Dickinson]. An exile without physical displacement; a going away without going away . . .

Yet home, too, is recognized as an ephemeral place—a temporary refuge— but one that is, over time, never the same, however much the longing for sameness; it is always seen as a place that is passing away. The real home—the only homeland Dickinson finds with conviction—is writing itself, poised as it is between a boundary-less heaven and no-heaven, the now and the infinite, disappointment and hoped-for fulfillment. Writing for Dickinson becomes an "imaginary homeland," the one true place a placeless place, a place of symbols running across the page . . .

The pain of separation in Dickinson's letters invariably opens up an agony of anticipation: a passion for an indivisible being that borders on the violent. Dickinson's voice speaks out of the desolation of a final abandonment, in a fever of pain and hoped-for ecstasy: "I need you more and more, and the great world grows wider, and dear ones fewer and fewer, every day that you stay away—I miss my biggest heart; my own goes wandering round and calls for Susie—Friends are too dear to sunder, Oh they are far too few, and how soon will they go away to where you and I cannot find them, *dont* let us forget these things, for their remembrance *now* will save us many an anguish when it is *too late* to love them! Susie, forgive me Darling, for every word I say—my heart is full of you, none other than you in my thoughts, yet when I seek to say to you something not for the world, words fail me. If you were here—and Oh that you were, my Susie, we need not talk at all, our eyes would whisper for us, and your hand held fast in mine, we would not ask for language—I try to bring you nearer, I chase the weeks away till they are quite departed, and fancy you have come, and I am on my way through the green lane to meet you, and my heart goes scampering so, that I have much ado to bring it back again, and learn it to be patient, til that dear Susie comes." [No. 94, 1852—to Susan Gilbert (Dickinson)] The longing here, as elsewhere, is for a communion of such intensity that language becomes superannuated, shed in favor of the more primal—and satisfying—physical language of touch and sight. Paradoxically, this longing is relayed in language.

Language as necessity: only it can make present, through symbol, what is absent, missed. To summon into being through a willfully rich and idiosyncratic language, that which is missed, that which is absent, that which is not there and will not be there, the elusive ideal that always escapes embodiment, that always escapes historical form—this is the American fate Dickinson shares with her predecessors and successors alike.

Like 'Bartleby,' Dickinson's writing dramatizes the horror of American individualism—in the most individual of terms. A horror that menaces reason and brings being to the threshold of madness. Madness that is its secret sharer. "I think of you dear Susie *now*, I dont know how or why, but more dearly as every day goes by, and that sweet month of promise draws nearer and nearer; and I view July so differently from I used to—once it seemed parched and dry—and I hardly loved it *any* on account of it's heat and dust; but *now* Susie, month of all the year the best; I skip the violets—and the dew, and early Rose and the Robins; I will exchange them *all* for that angry and hot noonday, when I can count the hours and the *minutes* before you come—Oh Susie, I often think I will try to tell you how very dear you are, and how I'm watching for you, but the words wont come, tho' the *tears* will, and I sit down disappointed—yet darling, you know it all—then why do I see to tell you? I do not know; in thinking of those I love my reason is all gone from me and I do fear sometimes that I must make a hospital for the hopelessly insane, and chain me up there such times, so I wont injure you ..." [No. 77, 1852—to Susan Gilbert (Dickinson)]

And within the cell of individualism, Dickinson's writing discovers vertiginous pleasures, pleasures that unmake the world.

The boon of language: "The boon of language is not tenderness. All that it holds, it holds with exactitude and without pity. Even a term of endearment: the term is impartial; the context is all. The boon of language is that potentially it is complete, it has the potentiality of holding with words the totality of human experience. Everything that has occurred and that may occur. It even allows space for the unspeakable. In this sense one can say of language that it is potentially the only human home, the only dwelling place that cannot be hostile to man. For prose this home is a vast territory, a country which it crosses through a network of tracks, paths, highways; for poetry this home is concentrated on a single centre, a single voice. [. . .] Every authentic poem contributes to the labour of poetry. And the task of this unceasing labour is to bring together what life has separated or violence has torn apart. Physical pain can usually be lessened or stopped by action. All other human pain, however, is caused by one form or another of human separation. And here the act of assuagement is less direct. Poetry can repair no loss, but it defies the space which separates. And it does this by its continual labour of reassembling what has been scattered." (John Berger, "The Hour of Poetry").

To quote Berger again: "Poetry makes language care because it renders everything intimate. This intimacy is the result of the poem's labour, the result of the bringing-together-intimacy of every act and every noun and event and perspective to which the poem refers. There is often nothing more substantial to place against the cruelty and indifference of the world than this caring.

From where does Pain come to us?
From where does he come?
He has been the brother of our visions
    from time immemorial
And the guide of our rhymes

Writes the Iraqi poet Nazik al-Mil'-ika." (John Berger, "The Hour of Poetry").

(But the boon of Dickinson's language is in no small part its tenderness—a tenderness replete with exactitude and pitiless—a fine measuring of affection calibrated to offset the emptiness of loss: "Could there be new tenderness, it would be for you, but the heart is full—another throb would split it—nor would we dare to speak to those whom such a grief removes, but we have somewhere heard "A little child shall lead them." [No. 729, 1881—to Mrs. J.G. Holland]. A tenderness that makes language care because it renders everything intimate).

"He has been the brother of our visions [. . .]": the harvesting of pain in Dickinson's writing brings an extraordinary clarity of *seeing*: everything seen at once in terms of the essential, "the" essential truth of a particular moment in history—its unremarked idiosyncrasy—but also the relevance of this historical moment for a transhistorical understanding. Dickinson's writing sees everything in terms of a double consciousness: the temporal perspective—the here-and-now, but the here-and-now seen from the perspective of one who is dead, or one who is swiftly approaching the threshold of death ("We too, are flying—fading, John—and the song "here lies," soon upon our lips that love us now—will have hummed and ended." [No. 184, 1856—to John L. Graves].) It is this double seeing that unexpectedly makes her work preternaturally aware of the distinctiveness of the temporal moment, of history in its moment of becoming. Dickinson in 1880: "Most of our Moments are Moments of Preface— "Seven Weeks" is a long Life—if it is all lived—" [No. 641, 1880—to T.W. Higginson]. Or, similarly, Dickinson in 1856: "My only sketch, profile, of Heaven is a large, blue sky bluer and larger than the *biggest* I have seen in June, and in it are my friends—all of them—every one of them—those who are with me now, and those who were "parted" as we walked, and "snatched up to Heaven."

Of roses had not faded, and frosts had never come, and one had not fallen here or there whom I could not waken, there were no need of other Heaven than the one below—and if God had been here this summer, and seen the things *I* have seen—I guess that He would think His paradise superfluous. Don't tell Him, for the world, though, for after all He's said about it, I should like to see what He *was* building for us, with no hammer, and no stone, and no journeyman either. Dear Mrs. Holland, I love to-night—love you and Dr. Holland, and "time and sense"—and fading things, and things that do *not* fade." [No. 185, 1856—to Mrs. J. G. Holland]

The Edenic: Dickinson's work gravitates toward imagery of Edenic innocence, but it simultaneously refuses to affirm them as adequate descriptions of the world. The reality of pain discomforts the easy consolations of any willed innocence. Rather, Dickinson's work incarnates a *radical* innocence, a sense of "History is what hurts" (Fredric Jameson).

Dickinsonian history: the history of the world *upon* the body (as translated into writing).

Or as Blanchot enjoins: "Learn to think with pain" (*The Writing of Disaster*). Pain makes possible Dickinson's gift of double consciousness— but at a price: "You need not fear to leave me lest I should be alone, for I often part with things I fancy I have loved, —sometimes to the grave, and sometimes to an oblivion rather bitterer that [sic] death—thus my heart bleeds so frequently that I shan't mind the hemorrhage, and I only add an agony to several previous ones, and at the end of day remark—a bubble burst! [. . .]

Sue—I have lived by this. It is the lingering emblem of the Heaven I once dreamed, and though if this is taken, I shall remain alone, and though in that last day, the Jesus Christ you love, remark he does not know me—there is a darker spirit will not disown its child.

Few have been given me, and if I love them so, that for *idolatry*, they are removed from me—I simply murmur *gone*, and the billow dies away into the boundless blue, and no one knows but me, that one went down today. We have walked very pleasantly—Perhaps this is the point at which our paths diverge—then pass on singing Sue, and up the distant hill I journey on." [No. 173, 1854—to Susan Gilbert (Dickinson)].

"Paradise is of the option." [No. 319, 1866—to T.W. Higginson]

The Master Letters

[I]

Dear Master,

I am ill, but grieving more that you are ill, I make my stronger hand work long eno' to tell you. I thought perhaps you were in Heaven, and when you spoke again, it seemed quite sweet, and wonderful, and surprised me so—I wish that you were well.

I would that all I love, should be weak no more. The Violets are by my side, the Robin very near, and "Spring"—they say, Who is she—going by the door—

Indeed it is God's house—and these are the gates of Heaven, and to and fro, the angels go, with their sweet postillions—I wish that I were great like Mr. Michael Angelo, and could paint for you. You ask me what my flowers said—then they were disobedient—I gave them messages. They said what the lips in the West, say, when the sun goes down, and so says the Dawn.

Listen again, Master. I did not tell you that today had been the Sabbath Day.

Each Sabbath on the Sea, makes me count the Sabbaths, till we meet on shore—and (will the) whether the hills will look as blue as the sailors say. I cannot talk any more (stay any longer) tonight (now), for this pain denies me.

How strong when weak to recollect, and easy, quite, to love. Will you tell me, please to tell me, soon as you are well." [No. 187, about 1858—*To recipient unknown*]

The address to an unidentified Master is an address to a longing that cannot be fulfilled. The desire: to be *ruled*, mastered, but redemptively, beyond the ordinary logic of subordination: to be subordinated to desire and at the same time to be imperious in addressing it— in a deliberately disheveled language, that is, in a language that will not be *mastered*.

The mystery of the Master letters: more important than the mystery of the addressee is the recognition that they are addressed to "Master," to mastery itself, and are dramatic enactments, workings out in the moment of composition, of Dickinson's Delphic relation to mastery, a condition that is not synonymous with desire, poetry, language, authority or tradition, but imbricated in all of them in such labyrinthine ways that in addressing any one, she addresses them all. The elusiveness of these letters is due in part to the fluidity of desire in them, for Dickinson refuses the position of the subject before the master, the relationship of the initiate who serves the master, and instead aspires to occupy both positions at once, or to move with unaccustomed freedom between them, according to an epochal imperative of the *moment* . . .

The visionary: faith in that which is beyond sight: "The Sailor cannot see the North—but knows the Needle can—" [No. 265, 1862—to T.W. Higginson. That is, the vanishing of the real, the disinheritance of custom and convention—which is the inauguration of a new ceremony.

Pain and the visionary: *I cannot talk any more (stay any longer) tonight (now), for this pain denies me.* The body in pain, but pain brought to the threshold of ecstasy. Indeed, the body is signified only through pain that is a portal to ecstasy. The diminishment of bodily power brings with it an attendant amplification of emotional intensity that trembles at the outer edge of visionary experience. The body in pain is embraced inasmuch as while it saps strength, it also renders her one with "Master"—a state of being that is exhausting *and* triumphant.

Desire that runs off the page . . . Dickinson's fervent language must recreate the world to simply express itself. In Dickinson's letter, the world is burdened with a richness of meaning that only metaphor can begin to approximate: "that things only seem to be things" (Henry Reed, "Judging Distances"). This is the *wilderness* of Dickinson's writing in which metaphor possesses at least as much substance as the reality that it stands in for; indeed it *transforms* the inhabited world. Language brings Dickinson to the threshold of the ineffable, to an epiphanic vision of desire fulfilled. In this sense, the letter itself—language—is "God's house": "We read the words but know them not." [No. 729, 1881—to Mrs. J.G. Holland]

To approach language for Dickinson is to approach the threshold of the unsayable: "The broadest words are so narrow we can easily cross them—but there is water deeper than those which has no Bridge." [No. 413, 1874—to T.W. Higginson]. The fear here is the fear of arresting the world in a language that reduces it, that makes it simple, singular, straightforward: "You remember the imperceptible has no external Face." [No. 391, 1873—to Mrs. J. G. Holland]. Dickinson's language always resists the commonsensical, "the evident." The self-evident: the most sinister of all myths.

"I gave them messages." In this Master Letter, Nature is made to participate in language—a role it apparently resists—but even what the messages articulate is ineffable. We witness here the reported speech of the visionary in which self and world are no longer sundered, but articulate, one, animate, *conjoined*: "The war is over says the river, the stars are all in me" (Jorie Graham, "Emergency")

"Nature is a Haunted House—but Art—a House that tries to be haunted." [No. 459a, 1876—to T.W Higginson]. How to write in such a way that the mysteries of existence are preserved; how to write in such a way that what is written maintains the enigma of life? Not art reflecting reality, but art trying to live up to the ineffable mystery of reality. Mimesis: the dead letter.

"The novel is the epic of the world abandoned by God"—Lukács; Dickinson's letters and poems—also epics of a world haunted by God . . .

[II]
Master,

If you saw a bullet hit a Bird—and he told you he was'nt shot—you might weep at his courtesy, but you would certainly doubt his word.

One drop more from the gash that stains your Daisy's bosom—then would you *believe*? Thomas' faith in Anatomy, was stronger than his faith in faith. God made me— [Sir] Master—I did'nt be—myself. I dont know how it was done. He built the heart in me—Bye and bye it outgrew me— and like the little mother—with the big child—I got tired holding him. I heard of a thing called "Redemption"—which rested men and women. You remember I asked you for it—you gave me something else. I forgot the Redemption [in the Redeemed—I didn't tell you for a long time, but I knew you had altered me—I] and was tired—no more— [so dear did this stranger become that were it, or my breath—the Alternative—I had tossed the fellow away with a smile.] I am older—tonight, Master—but the love is the same—so are the moon and the crescent. If it had been God's will that I might breathe where you breathed—and find the place—myself—at night—if I (can) never forget that I am not with you—and that sorrow and frost are nearer than I—if I wish with a might I cannot repress—that mine were the Queen's place—the love of the Plantagenet is my only apology—To come nearer than presbyteries—and nearer than the new Coat—that the Tailor made—the prank of the Heart at play on the Heart—in holy Holiday—is forbidden me—You make me say it over—I fear you laugh—when I do not see— [but] "Chillon" is not funny. Have you the heart in your breast—Sir—is it set like mine—a little to the left—has it the misgiving—if it wake in the night—perchance—itself to it—a timbrel is it—itself to it a tune?

These things are [reverent] holy, Sir, I touch them [reverently] hallowed, but persons who pray—dare remark [our] "Father"! You say I do not tell you all—Daisy confessed—and denied not.

Vesuvius dont talk—Etna dont— [Thy] one of them—said a syllable—a thousand years ago, and Pompeii heard it, and hid forever—She could'nt look the world in the face, afterward, I suppose—Bashful Pompeii! "Tell you of the want"—you know what a leech is, don't you—and [remember that] Daisy's arm is small—and you have felt the horizon hav'nt you—and did the sea—never come so close as to make you dance?

I dont know what you can do for it—thank you—Master—but if I had the Beard on my cheek—like you—and you—had Daisy's petals—and you cared so for me—what would become of you? Could you forget me in fight, or flight—or the foreign land? Couldn't Carlo, and you and I walk in the meadows an hour—and nobody care but the Bobolink—and *his*—a *silver* scruple? I used to think when I died—I could see you—so I died as fast as I could—but the "Corporation" are going to heaven too so [Eternity] wont be sequestered—now [at all]—Say I may wait for you—say I need go with no stranger to the to me—untried [country] fold—I waited a long time—Master—but I can wait no more—wait till my hazel hair is dappled—and you carry the cane—then I can look at my watch—and if the Day is too far declined—we can take the chances [of] for Heaven—What would you do with me if I came "in white?" Have you the little chest to put the Alive—in?

I want to see you more—Sir—than all I wish for in this world—and the wish—altered a little—will be my only one for the skies.

Could you come to New England— [this summer—could] would you come to Amherst—would you like to come—Master?

[Would it do harm—yet we both fear God—] Would Daisy disappoint you—no—she would'nt—Sir—if it were comfort forever—just to look in your face, while you looked in mine—then I could play in the woods till Dark—till you take me where Sundown cannot find us—and the true keep coming—till the town is full. [Will you tell me if you will?]

I did'nt think to tell you, you did'nt come to me "in white," nor ever told me why,

No rose, yet felt myself a' bloom,

No bird—yet rode in Ether.

[No. 233, about 1861—*To recipient unknown*]

Who is the "I" that wrote this letter? Who is the "I" that writes these lines? The self as other—and more various than the signs used to signify it. Dickinson's writing: an affront to the forgeries of bourgeois order. *As if the world was transparent, a set of givens, universally-agreed upon . . .* "Who are you to live in all these many forms?" (Terrence Malick, *The Thin Red Line*). Dickinson: "How can I not live in all these many forms"?

The letter as violence (the opening of the wound): but also, the letter as ecstatic vision, as elegy, as promise, as promissory note . . . the feverish search for figures to express the inexpressible: the drama of being *unselved* protracted to an almost unbearable extent.

It is the pitilessness & ferocity of Dickinson's *seeing*, of her knowledge of the laws of necessity, her clarity, that gives her writing its stringency, its awful power to unsettle; a seeing that transgresses the usual boundary between subject and object: "but which was the Child of Fiction, the Child of Fiction or of Fact, and is "Come unto me" for Father or Child, when the Child precedes?" [No. 653, 1880—to T.W. Higginson]

The letter as elegy: memorial for the self that could not be.

To whom or what may I turn and where will that turning bring? For Dickinson, the question of audience is nothing less than a question of being; one kind of audience creates one kind of being, the lack of it, another. Within that situation, writing allows for another kind of self-fashioning.

"The world in its worlding." Only experience defined by intense pain—despair, un-fulfillment, mortal disappointment—could give rise to the ecstatic re-visioning of the Master letters, a transubstantiation of language that opens up new worlds—as well as being a leave-taking of some old ones.

The Master letters: ecstatic visions of, and invitations to, a future union, necessarily postponed . . .

To write ecstatically, without an audience, without the expectation of an audience, without the expectation of being heard or understood, but with fearlessness & revolutionary power—this is the American legacy Dickinson inherited, received, & rewrote . . .

The most innovative literary texts are those little or no audience. All great pioneering texts share the same situation: the lack of an audience and the—imagined—need for one.

At its most intense, as in the Master Letters, Dickinson's writing never mimics the world. Worldliness never enters in that way. Rather, worldliness is detectable in the figures of her language, in her forms . . . the world *ghosts* her art, and its haunting is as real as any specter.

Ecstasy here is the only redemption: an ecstasy of language, of imaginative power, that glancingly touches upon the world, an ecstasy no less concerned with its own salvation, its own figuration—its own *transfiguration*—than the failed and fallen world that gives rise to it.

Out of that desire to transfigure a failed and fallen world the word is opened to the play of metaphor. The violence of Dickinson's metaphors testifies to the rifts of this world—its "terrible beauty" . . .

Violence as the guarantor of belief; the maker of true believers.

American history: the reiteration of a "violence narrative" in which violence is employed to make believers out of unbelievers; violence used to sanctify the cause. Dickinson invokes this tradition— "One drop more from the gash that stains your Daisy's bosom—then would you *believe?*"—to suggest its power, *and* its impoverishment . . .

The violence of the unsaid, the violence of the said: "Vesuvius dont talk—Etna dont—[Thy] one of them—said a syllable—a thousand years ago, and Pompeii heard it, and hid forever—." Speaking as eruption, the transformation comes from pent-up energy suddenly released: the *rush* of language. This is true, even while the speaking takes place without an audience. At the very least, speaking can transform the speaker and the world in which he or she finds him/herself . . . merely to *say* it, even in an unsent letter, can change one's relation to the world, can change the world as the writer knows it.

Writing as waiting, constant waiting: "Loss goes with writing" (Maurice Blanchot).

The seduction of death: death as longed-for release from the carceral self, death as communion, as the intermingling of souls. Death as a beginning, not an end. Death glimpsed in writing, in the loss that "goes with" writing. But the loss that goes with writing is also a triumph: the triumphant prefiguring of death, and the hope for a new sovereignty—the much-desired and deferred state of bliss, undiminished. Writing is the fragile instrument for this hope.

[III]
To recipient unknown
    "Oh, did I offend it— [Did'nt it want me to tell it the truth] Daisy—Daisy—offend it—who bends her smaller life to his (it's) meeker (lower) every day—who only asks—a task—[who] something to do for love of it—some little way she cannot guess to make that master glad—
    A love so big it scares her, rushing among her small heart—pushing aside the blood and leaving her faint (all) and white in the gust's arm—

Daisy—who never flinched thro' that awful parting, but held her life so tight he should not see the wound—who would have sheltered him in her childish bosom (Heart)—only it was'nt big eno' for a Guest so large—*this* Daisy—grieve her Lord—and yet it (she) often blundered—Perhaps she grieved (grazed) his taste—perhaps her odd—Backwoodsman [life] ways [troubled] teased his finer nature (sense). Daisy [fea] knows all that—but must she go unpardoned—teach her, preceptor grace—teach her majesty—Slow (Dull) at patrician things—Even the wren upon her nest learns (knows) more than Daisy dares—

Low at the knee that bore her once unto [royal] wordless rest [now] Daisy [stoops] kneels a culprit—tell her her [offence] fault—Master—if it is [not so] small eno' to cancel with her life, [Daisy] she is satisfied—but punish [do not] dont banish her—shut her in prison, Sir—only pledge that you will forgive—sometime—before the grave, and Daisy will not mind—she will awaken in [his] your likeness.

Wonder stings me more than the Bee—who never did sting me—but made gay music with his might wherever I [may] [should] go—Wonder wastes my pound, you said I had no size to spare—

You send the water over the Dam in my brown eyes—

I've got a cough big as a thimble—but I dont care for that—I've got a Tomahawk in my side but that dont hurt me much. [If you] Her master stabs her more—

Wont he come to her—or will he let her seek him, never minding [whatever] so long wandering [out] if to him at last.

Oh how the sailor strains, when his boat is filling—Oh how the dying tug, till the angel comes. Master—open your life wide, and take me in forever, I will never be tired—I will never be noisy when you want to be still. I will be [glad] [as the] your best little girl—nobody else will see me, but you—that is enough—I shall not want any more—and all that Heaven only will disappoint me—will be because it's not so dear."

The fevered isolation of this letter echoes through subsequent generations of American writing. Recall Eliot: "Speak to me. Why do you never speak. Speak./ 'What are you thinking of? What thinking? What?/ 'I never know what you are thinking. Think." ('The Waste Land'). The American genius for isolation matures a strange, rare—and desperate—variety of desire. Desire that cleaves the self, transfigures the word and seeks, in its desperation, to transfigure the world. The elegy of the invocation to the other, the other who is silent, who does not speak, cannot speak, but whose presence is nonetheless acutely felt: the terrible distance, is equal only to the terrible proximity, the imagined proximity, of the object of desire. The Master letters are also an elegy to the self, marooned between the flesh-self, and the word-self, each isolate, each desiring a consummation beyond the self . . .

Dickinson's American machismo. The lover to her beloved, with the machismo of the Indian fighter: "but I dont care for that—I've got a Tomahawk in my side but that dont hurt me much.": the *American* bravado of it! Violence as love, love as violence—the wound as the emblem of faithfulness, the token of fidelity. The violent penetration of the body as the sign of love: only a frontier culture, persuaded of its righteousness, accustomed to conquest, and the strange intimacies of blood-letting, could so confuse love and violence.

William Carlos Williams: "Never mind; the great event may not exist, so there is no need to speak further of it. Kill! Kill! the English, the Irish, the French, the Germans, the Italians and the rest: friends or enemies, it makes no difference, kill them all. The bridge is to blown up when all Russia is upon it. And why?
     Because we love them—all." (*Spring and All*)

Pain: the only felt connection to the impossible: hence the prolonged dwelling in its domain, and Dickinson's embrace of it.

Wonder at the hugeness of the world; its perfidy, its painfulness—and no escape, at least not this side of death. This is the wonder, the astonishment, at the core of the Master Letters. Revelation as inauguration into pain, undreamt of levels of suffering. The basis of Dickinson's visionary writing is a refusal to normalize pain, a refusal to become hardened to it, a refusal to become socialized into insensitivity. The radical innocence of Dickinson's writing comes at the cost of a willingness to *flinch*, to remain open—at all cost— to pain (which is itself an intrepid openness to the world).

Wound: the invisible opening. The rending of the spirit's flesh. Spelled out, disclosed (withheld) in letters. Unanswered, unanswerable. Undiscloseable. Writing as *stigmata*. The opened up body, the flailed body. The body that cannot be exposed, cannot be made an object of compassion, cannot be made an object of the physician's ministry of hand and eye. Made to wear the dress of normalcy, as if the red openings into flesh were not. Tyranny of invisible wounds, the tyranny of the body made invisible. The body as sacrifice. Sacrificial body. Dressed up in white, as whiteness. Whiteness. Witness. Someone else to witness? Not even widow's weeds. Whiteness as blackness. Whiteness as whiteness, dazzlingly ambiguous . . . the awful whiteness, unspotted . . .

Edmond Jabès: "In breaking the silence, language realizes what silence wanted and could not obtain, "writes Merleau-Ponty. So it is out of breakage—breakage in death, of death—but of the fatal fissure that rends it mortal while bringing it about, that the question of the book is born. Question put to nothingness, to the void. Question of the void around which swarm mad words that, though impotent, are yet master of the question."

Dickinson's writing: a fascicle of pain, hand-sewn, threaded with hope (and no hope), *yet master of the question* (and everywhere, silence, "that Pause of Space") [No. 418, 1874—to T. W. Higginson].

The author as writer, character and audience: "This is my letter to the World/That never wrote to Me—." A new language is made possible by this isolation, forged in, and out of, it; but Dickinson's work—like Wallace Stevens'— attends equally to the ironies of the *cost* of that refinement of the dialect of the tribe. Consider the last half or so of Stevens' "A Postcard from the Volcano":

        [. . .] and the windy sky

Cries out a literate despair.
We knew for long the mansion's look
And what we said of it became

A part of what it is . . . Children,
Still weaving budded aureoles,
Will speak our speech and never know,

Will say of the mansion that it seems
As if he that lived there left behind
A spirit storming in blank walls,

A dirty house in a gutted world,
A tatter of shadows peaked to white,
Smeared with the gold of the opulent sun.

The literate despair comes not from the windy sky but from the "literate-ness" of the speaker, from the new language s/he has contrived to invent (though the despair is such it seems to come from the sky itself). One of the costs of this refinement is the cost of misunderstanding the creators of the mansion: they are imprisoned by their creation, imprisoned by the language they use, even as it enables the world they inhabit. The poet is the "spirit storming in blank walls"— and because of it, transformed, but also transformed into caricature. The problem is not that the language is entirely lost to the tribe, but that it is not *known* to it. Its potentiality: lost—or stricken . . .

For the American writer, estrangement is the condition responsible for the tradition of idiosyncratic writing, for the existence of "the mansion": it is both "A dirty house in a gutted world" and one "Smeared with the gold of the opulent sun." Enabling impoverishment: the condition that defines the fate of American writing.

The position of the American writer "storming in blank walls" informs the perennial American aspiration to write the unreadable text, which is, in its own way, an invitation to an *engagement* extended to an imagined community (as well as being an act of defiance): "I have met no othe [rs.]" [No. 249, 1862—to Samuel Bowles].

Hence the ambiguity of her position! "Oh nation of the soul thou hast thy freedom now." [No. 559, 1878—to Otis P. Lord]

Questions of faith: in Dickinson's letters, faith is largely a question of faithfulness, which translates into a question of relationship, and the intensity of the relationship. How to be faithful to others who may not reciprocate? Dickinson's letters demand much, but offer much; indeed, they are distinguished by a purity of devotion, religious in its intensity:

"You must let me go first, Sue, because I live in the Sea always and know the Road.
I would have drowned twice to save you sinking, dear, If I could only have covered your Eyes so you would'nt have seen the Water." [No. 306, 1865—to Susan Gilbert Dickinson]

Yet faith and faithfulness do not belong exclusively to notions of friendship, or even the soul; they are the binding elements of community, dependent as it is upon a reciprocity that exceeds human failure. Dickinson's writing desires to keep faith with the imaginary community that she bodies forth in language. This community is less an articulated vision than a gnomic grammar of affirmations in which the imperatives of a commercial economy are superannuated in favor of those of an economy of art. In this economy, *feeling-as-thought* becomes purified and intensified through a mastery of form. (It may be that this economy of art is "unreal," but it is no less strange, no less real, than the market economies ruled by normalized disfiguration, normalized inequality . . .).

The palimpsestic world: for Dickinson the world is the signified world; it *is* always already being revised, rewritten. "This World is not Conclusion" [P501] because of "A Species [that] stands beyond—" but also because the world is always in *flux*, working toward different conclusions. Dickinson's letters: testimonies to wonder, seen and found. In continually affirming the inseparability of life from the writing of it, signs themselves become wondrous, plenipotentiaries of the endlessness of expressive understanding in the face of necessity, death, and with all that is resistant to imaginative seeing: "I can scarcely believe that the Wondrous Book is at last to be written, and it seems like a Memoir of the Sun, when the Noon is gone—" [No. 908, 1884—to Susan Gilbert Dickinson]

Yet always the radical innocence, the revolutionary's consciousness, the refusal to accept the given as inevitable, as *only* that: "Which Earth are we in?" [No. 750, 1882—to Otis P. Lord]. Which is to say, her refusal to accept "the Treason of an Accent."

(Dickinson's letters: a Wondrous Book, the pages of which are still turning, looking to resurrect a world that trembles just beyond sight. Across the generations, Dickinson's vision haunts us, reminds us that America is also "like a Memoir of the Sun, when the Noon is gone," but a memoir whose final pages have yet to be written . . .)

Chapter 5
Michael Herr's *Dispatches*:
Ferocious Alphabets

"Whatever is done from love always occurs beyond good and evil."
—Nietzsche

Dispatches: the most curious of love letters . . .

But also, an elegiac state-of-the-union meditation on violence and language in the high noon of an imperial quagmire. Hence the willingness to be painfully self-revelatory. Hence the anger at the betrayal, among other things, of a common language. *Dispatches* sees the violence of language, the violence of the letter, the letter that kills, the language that effaces, euphemizes, vaporizes. Dispatches: sendings off, communications, executions—all share a common denominator: death. For to send away (exile, reject, conscript), to write an official report, can involve a form of death as sure as execution, if not as obvious . . .

The violence of the letter that legitimizes killing to the extent that death becomes a rhetorical figure, doomed to stand in for a reality it cannot signify. *Dispatches* autopsies the effects of killing, pinpoints causes, especially the language that kills. The letter as violent, the letter that wars against violence . . . in a culture of death, the letter takes on a deathly urgency, a deathly aura.

But the letter also takes on an urgency charged with the pure vitality of life, never more alive than in its last flare-up of incandescent beauty and terror.

Vietnam as a swarm of texts; texts thick as flies. Letters, reports, statements, newspaper articles, write-ups, announcements, cover-ups, communiques, investigations, circulars, memos, maps, mimeographs, photographs, photocopies, poems, duplicates, facsimiles, tallies, stories, songs: all *dispatches* of one kind or another. All *letters*. Recall 'Bartleby': "Dead letters. Does it not sound like dead men?"

How can letters be violent? When they kill, lead men to their deaths, then euphemize those deaths—is that not proof of their violence? (As if proof would be sufficient). The violence of the letter, yes, but also its ferocity, "ferocious alphabets": language as the site of violence, war—and its resistance. Scarlet letters redux.

"Nothing so horrible ever happened upcountry that it was beyond language fix and press relations, a squeeze fit into the computers would make the heaviest numbers jump up and dance. You'd either meet an optimism no violence could unconvince or a cynicism that would eat itself empty every day and then turn, hungry and malignant, on whatever it could for a bite, friendly or hostile, it didn't matter. Those men called dead Vietnamese "believers," a lost American platoon was "a black eye," they talked as if killing a man was nothing more than depriving him of his vigor."

Lying always runs the risk that the liar will come to believe his lie. When that happens, the liar *loses* the world, and cannot distinguish himself from an angel or a devil. This fatal wishful thinking is what befell the military brass in Vietnam—and in part, America itself: "A twenty-four-year old Special Forces captain was telling me about it: I went out and killed one VC and liberated a prisoner. Next day the major called me in and told me that I killed fourteen VC and liberated six prisoners. You want to see the medal?" The need for America to always be *good* is deeply rooted in Americans (since the Puritans, we have been a uniquely "good" people; necessarily good because we were a *chosen* people); hence the seductions, and perils, of lying to ourselves as a nation.

If Sir Walter Scott's romantic fiction led to the Civil War, as some have claimed, then movies, especially Westerns and war flicks, can be said to have played a part in the Vietnamese war. "I keep thinking about all the kids who got wiped out by seventeen years of war movies before coming to Vietnam to get wiped out for good. You don't know what a media freak is until you've seen the way a few of those grunts would run around during a fight when they knew that there was a television crew nearby; they were actually making war movies in their heads, doing little guts-and-glory Leatherneck tap dances under fire, getting their pimples shot off for the networks. They were insane, but the war hadn't done that to them. Most combat troops stopped thinking of the war as an adventure after the first few firefights, but there were always the ones who couldn't let that go, these few who were up there doing numbers for the cameras. A lot of correspondents weren't much better. We'd all seen too many movies, stayed too long in Television City, years of media glut had made certain connections difficult. The first few times that I had got fired at or saw combat deaths, nothing had really happened, all the responses got locked in my head. It was the same familiar violence only moved over to another medium: some kind of jungle play with giant helicopters and fantastic special effects, actors lying out there in canvas body bags waiting for the scene to end so they could get up again and walk it off. But that was some scene (you found out), there was no cutting it.

A lot of things had to be unlearned before you could learn anything at all, and even after you knew better you couldn't avoid the ways in which things got mixed, the war itself with those parts of the war that were just like the movies, just like *The Quiet American* or *Catch-22* [. . .]." America's fate: to be powerful—and trapped in the funhouse of its own mythologies.

In Herr's book, Vietnam is both a text and a not-text. Yet the text *wills* the not-text into being, gives violent birth to a new Vietnam, one that heartlessly replaces the old.

Maps, mapping, ground: The coordinates of a reality that is never *there*. Wasn't that the problem "with" Vietnam? That our representation of it never corresponded with the reality? That America tried to create a Vietnam suasive to its own desires—one that Vietnam rejected, ultimately *expelled*? Vietnam during the "Vietnamese" war: a bastard simulacrum, orphaned now in history's vast orphanage . . . "You'd stand nailed there in your tracks, sometimes, no bearings and none in sight, thinking, *Where the fuck am I*, having fallen into some unnatural East/West interface, a California corridor cut and bought and burned deep into Asia, and once we'd done it, we couldn't remember what for. It was axiomatic that it was about ideological space, we were there to bring them the choice, bringing it to them like Sherman bringing the Jubilee through Georgia, clean through it, wall to wall with pacified indigenous and scorched earth."

What do maps map if not the ground? Are they even real? "That map was a marvel, especially since it wasn't real anymore [...] The paper had buckled in its frame after years in the wet Saigon heat, laying a kind of veil over the countries it depicted. Vietnam was divided into its older territories of Tonkin, Annam and Cochin China, and to the west, past Laos and Cambodge sat Siam, a kingdom. That's old, I'd tell visitors, that's a really old map." Can it be that they map out nothing more than the kingdom of our desires, our wish to make the world transparent, knowable, known? The wish to remake the strangeness of the world in our own image is manifest in what they leave out. They purge reality of difference. The *absence* of reality is what makes maps the same everywhere. At the same time, the thin blue lines follow the trace of wishes we hardly know how to speak of. This is what makes them *marvelous* . . .

Hence the nostalgia evoked by old maps: it is the nostalgia for an older set of desires, desires that have become quaint with age, sepia-toned, brittle, distant from contemporary maps which purport to replicate the real, inscribing it within a labyrinth of lines. Renaissance maps illustrated monsters rearing up out of ocean foam at the edge of the world; from the beginning, the connection between maps and the monstrous was made manifest. Today's maps do not show monsters; *they* are monstrous.

The history of maps is a history of desire.

All maps lay a veil over the countries they depict.

Maps: war by other means.

The American presence in Vietnam: *groundless*. Hence the mania for maps.

The destruction of the Ho Bo Woods and many other jungles in Vietnam: the revenge of the West upon the East for presuming to be *different*.

In the American, Puritan-derived consciousness, the jungle is affiliated with the wilderness, an ungodly, heathenish unmapped territory associated with the dark places of the mind. Mary Rowlandson: "I went along that day mourning and lamenting, leaving farther my own country, and traveling into a vast and howling wilderness, and I understood something of Lot's wife's temptation, when she looked back." In eradicating the jungle, the attempt was to eradicate fear, the unknown, fear of the unknown, indeed the unconsciousness itself. *If only Vietnam could be mapped, seen, made visible, made an object of complete surveillance, then the war could be won.*

Dominion—the American obsession. Is there a greater one? "Once it was all locked in place, Khe San became like the planted jar in Wallace Stevens' poem. It took dominion everywhere." The jar defines the wilderness as wilderness; in its very arbitrariness, it creates a centered, geographical space—it takes dominion everywhere just as Khe San, the doomed American outpost in Vietnam "took dominion everywhere." Or sought to. Herr's quotation of Stevens' "Anecdote of a Jar" subtly touches upon the long history of conquest in the New World which worked by a process of redefinition of geographical space—the creation of new centers in the "widerness"—with renamings of that space, just as Vietnam was renamed. The jar is other: "It did not give of bird or bush." Yet Stevens' poem gestures also to an ineluctable lesson of Vietnam (this is its genius; it can do this): however powerful any redefinition of geographical space, that new map, that redefinition, is also a fiction, a representation. And the siege at Khe San testifies to the perils of confusing representations with reality: that dominion—established by a jar or a base—can be redefined; it is not an integral part of nature. And when the military decided that Khe San, the western anchor of the war, wasn't that at all, and abandoned it, the fiction of dominion departed too, and the jungle returned. The wily minimalism of Stevens' tart anecdote suggests both the power and fragility of dominion (just as the jar, too, is a metaphor for poetry, and a cautionary tale on *its* aspirations to dominion, *its* power and fragility . . .)

The origin of the Vietnam War is itself a palimpsest in which layer upon layer of writing, of history, goes at least as far back as the domestication of the New World. Vietnam: not an aberration in American history, but a pure product of it: "You couldn't find two people who agreed about when it began, how could you say when it began going off? Mission intellectuals like 1954 as the reference date; if you saw back as far as War II and the Japanese occupation, you were practically a historical visionary.

"Realists" said that it began for us in 1961, and the common run of Mission flack insisted on 1965, post-Tonkin Resolution, as though all the killing that had gone before wasn't really war. Anyway, you couldn't use standard methods to date the doom; might as well say that Vietnam was where the Trail of Tears was headed all along, the turnaround point where it would touch and come back to form a containing perimeter; might just as well lay it on the proto-Gringos who found the New England woods too raw and empty for their peace and filled them up with their own imported devils."

Does all mythology emerge out of fear—fear of the unknown, fear of that which is different, empty, silent? Mythology, especially national mythology, works to eradicate difference, to transform that which is strange into that which is familiar: "the devil that you know . . ." In the New World, the besetting sin has always been the intolerance of difference: Eden could not be edenic precisely because it bad been cast into the role of being Eden.

Marx's dictum: "History repeats itself the first time as tragedy, the second time as farce." The tragic farce of American history is our amnesia, we repeat ourselves, our history, again and again, as if for the first time, with all the license of an innocent first embarking upon the world. Absolute innocence requires, too, an absolute form of amnesia, and amnesia is the price we pay for our innocence (and "innocence" is the price we pay for our amnesia).

Herr reminds us of the violence of the Vietnam War, but also the extreme righteousness with which it was prosecuted; the infallibility of the cause. In the righteousness of the violence that marked that war (and the denials and self-defensive justifications of it), we can see an affiliation between Vietnam and the eradication of indigenous peoples from the New World; both undertakings were underwritten by a belief in Manifest Destiny, which is itself but a new name for the righteousness the Puritans possessed, fortified as they were by the belief that they were fulfilling God's mission to create a New Jerusalem in the wilderness, to wrest a "shining city on the hill" out of the devil's territories. Violence on behalf of the sacred . . . and the sacred become violent. Which is not far off from the sacralization of violence.

What is the fate of irony in war? "'Come on,' the captain said, we'll take you to play Cowboys and Indians." We walked out from Song Be in a long line, maybe a hundred men; rifles, heavy automatics, mortars, portable one-shot rocked launchers, radios, medics; breaking into some kind of sweep formation, five files with small teams of specialists in each file. A gunship flew close hover-cover until we came to some low hills, then two more ships came along and peppered the hills until we'd passed safely through them. It was a beautiful operation. We played all morning until somebody on the point got something—a "scout," they thought, and then they didn't know. They couldn't even tell for sure whether he was from a friendly tribe or no, no markings on on his arrows because his quiver was empty, like his pockets and his hands." This finely-honed irony strikes out at the self-conscious/unself-conscious figuring of the Vietnam War as a re-enactment of *How The West Was Won*. There is a wink-and-a-nod to the ironies of restaging of the most famous ("colorful," "dramatic") chapter of American history—on Asian soil— but the significance of repeating genocide, or attempting to do so, circa the US in the 1960s, drops away, overtaken by the sheer excitement of war play. One play begets another: the extension of the Cowboy and Indian metaphor is allowed the full play of *its* grotesque implications in order to indicate the degree to which it has colonized our assumptions. Reality as theater, as an essentially histrionic process: the Vietnam War is made to become a re-enactment of the Cowboys and Indians myth. A diorama of history which has escaped the diorama. Here the Vietnamese man is forced into a Manichean allegory whereby he occupies the role of the (Indian) aggressor. Herr's language dramatizes the power of metaphor to metamorphose the actual (the Vietnamese man) into the allegorical (the Indian). More terrifying than the possibility that this man was an innocent is the realization that in this peculiar restaging of American myth, all that remains of him are metaphorical scraps.

To ironize catastrophe approaches futility; to not ironize it is to acquiesce in it. Irony: the necessary *first* gesture . . .

Conrad: "The conquest of the earth, which mostly means the taking of it away from those who have a different complexion or slightly flatter noses than ourselves, is not a pretty thing when you look into it too much. What redeems it is the idea only. An idea at the back of it; not a sentimental pretence but an idea; an unselfish belief in the idea—something you can set up, and bow down before, and offer a sacrifice to . . ." Herr has fewer illusions: the idea, for him, is ruinous, not redemptive. In the context of conquest, irony can no longer afford the luxury of outright self-contradiction.

No empire thinks of itself as an empire; it is always something else, something benign, ultimately, an expression of love. Nietzsche: "One has watched life badly if one has not also seen the hand that considerately—kills." (*Beyond Good and Evil*)

Dispatches: A lover's discourse, full of ambivalence toward his beloved.

The tragic achievement of a frontier nation is that it must continually *invent* new frontiers. Woe betide that which inhabits the space of the new frontier.

Vietnam: both not-home and not-foreign, a fast-forwarded, on-speed, colonial hybrid that never took hold. What could be more unsettling than something half a world away being half familiar—and wholly strange?

In Vietnam, the American obsession with mobility—mobility as the guarantor of individual freedom, mobility as self-expression, mobility as self-improvement—was rehearsed with a vengeance within the theater of war. Far from being a means of progress, it hastened a slow, inexorable process of disintegration: "Best way's to keep moving," one of them told us. "Just keep moving, stay in motion, you know what I'm saying?"

We knew. He was a moving-target-survivor-subscriber, a true child of the war, because except for rare times when you were pinned or stranded the system was geared to keep you mobile, if that was what you thought you wanted. As a technique for staying alive it seemed to make as much sense as anything, given naturally that you were there to begin with and wanted to see it close; it started out sound and straight but it formed a cone as it progressed, because the more you moved the more you saw, the more you saw the more besides death and mutilation you risked, and the more you risked of that, the more you would have to let go of one day as a "survivor." Some of us moved around the war like crazy people until we couldn't see which way the run was taking us anymore, only the war all over its surface with occasional, unexpected penetration." Mobility as death, or worse than death: the "moving-target-survivor-subscriber" risks psychosis. In Herr's Vietnam, there are no survivors. Atomized warfare, atomized bodies, atomized minds: "the system was geared to keep you mobile, if that was what you thought you wanted." Here rationality—or belief in rationality—leads to the breakdown of the man-machine at its most vulnerable. Vietnam as America's future . . .

Vietnam: mobility as catastrophe, the end of freedom, the death of freedom, the quintessence of unfreedom: the unbearable lightness of being.

Vietnam: the ruin of system; or, system's ruin revealed.

If we had let Vietnam signify itself, name itself, choose its own identity, there would have been no Vietnamese War (in Vietnam: "the American War"). The semantic fracturing of North and South Vietnam made war inevitable, and it maintained its necessity . . .

Vietnam: the culmination of the American pursuit to perfect the seamless integration of the man-in-the-machine, the man-as-machine. Fordism brought to new heights: the old illusion, the technological Holy Grail: the eradication of the human. (This is the fantasy of much of post-Vietnam science-fiction Hollywood, which thrives on post-apocalyptic scenarios). Vietnam: our first science-fiction war, our first truly spectacular war, the first war to become a widely seen, on-the-spot, televised spectacle. But Vietnam also dramatized the age-old Puritan refusal to see the dystopia borne out of the dream of a utopia. But also the terrifying/ exhilarating pleasure/pain seduction of dystopia. Was it really about winning or losing? When did it become something other than a conventional war? About pushing the technological envelope, *seeing what happens*? What could be *gotten away* with? "In the months after I got back the hundreds of helicopters I'd flown in began to draw together until they formed a collective meta-chopper, and in my mind, it was the sexiest thing going; saver-destroyer, provider-waster, right-hand, left-hand, nimble, fluent, canny and human; hot-steel, grease, jungle-saturated canvas webbing, sweat cooling and warming up again, cassette rock and roll in one ear and door-gun fire in the other, fuel, heat, vitality and death, death itself, hardly an intruder."

War as narcotic, a death-giving, death-defying unscrambling, repro-gramming *pleasure* machine: "'Quaking and Shakin','" they called it, great balls of fire, Contact. Then it was you and the ground: kiss it, eat it, fuck it, plow it with your whole body, get as close to it as you can without being in it yet or of it, guess who's flying around about an inch above your head? Pucker and submit, it's the ground. Under Fire would take you out of your head and your body too, the space you'd seen a second ago between subject and object wasn't there anymore, it banged shut in a fast wash of adrenaline. Amazing, unbelievable, guys who'd played a lot of hard sports said that they'd never felt anything like it, the sudden drop and rocket rush of the hit, the reserves of adrenaline you could make available to yourself, pumping it up and putting it out until you were lost floating in it, not afraid, almost open to clear orgasmic death-by-drowning in it, actually relaxed. Unless of course you'd shit your pants or were screaming or praying or giving anything at all to the hundred-channel panic that blew word salad all around you and sometimes clean through you. Maybe you couldn't love the war and hate it inside the same instant, but sometimes those feelings alternated so rapidly that they spun together in a strobic wheel rolling all the way up until you were literally High On War, like it said on all the helmet covers. Coming off a jag like that could really make a mess out of you." War as orgasm: never more alive than at the brink of death or dismemberment. No subject, no object—only is-ness—a perverse, amped mimicry of the tranquility of the Buddhist monks who gave themselves up to flames, their serenity a testament to a subjectless, objectless world, the violence of the flames a protest against human violence, a protest against the demonic pleasures of war.

Their *pain* a testament against the demonic pleasures of war . . .

War: the triumph of being—and its undoing.

War: the undoing of being—and its reincarnation, one way or another.

Maps, mapping, ground: —"There was a famous story, some reporters asked a door gunner, "How can you shoot women and children?" and he'd answered, "It's easy, you just don't lead 'em so much." Well, they said you needed a sense of humor, there you go, even the VC had one. Once after an ambush that killed lots of Americans, they covered the field with copies of a photograph that showed one more dead American, with the punch line mimeographed on the back, "Your X-rays have just come back from the lab and we think we know what the problem is."" Among other things, this "bad joke" is a black parody on the American reliance upon technology, upon its presumptive power to resolve all situations, cure all ills. The parody's twisted—but brutally effective—message is that this technology, and the presumption of God-like omniscience and righteousness that goes along with those who wield it, is deathly, creates death, produces dead bodies. The VC text is x-raying the American body politic, ruthlessly revealing the bad politics "behind" its techno-fantasies, its technology-driven will-to-power . . .

The proof of the body as body and not simply machine is not the dead body, but the presence of death, the dead. "Men on the crews would say that once you'd carried a dead person he would always be there, riding with you. Like all combat people they were incredibly superstitious and invariably self-dramatic, but it was (I knew) unbearably true that close exposure to the dead sensitized you to the force of their presence and made for long reverberations: long." The dead as *presence*. Their presence, their palpable presence, haunts the text of *Dispatches*, haunts all its texts, all its intertexts, calling into question the forced, victory-is-at-hand rhetoric until the irony it evoked became palpable, embarrassing, intolerable. Vietnam has always been a country that has reverenced the dead; in *Dispatches*, it is a ghostly country in every sense of the word (also America's ghost). It can be said, however, that those ghosts brought the war to an end.

Only the dead offer stories without rhetoric: "After a year I felt so plugged in to all the stories and the images and the fear that even the dead started telling me stories, you'd hear them out of a remote but accessible space where there were no ideas, no emotions, no facts, no proper language, only clean information. However many times it happened, whether I'd

114

known them or not, no matter what I'd felt about them, or the way they died, their story was always there and it was always the same: it went, "Put yourself in my place." America needs these rhetoric-less stories, even if they must take on the dress of rhetoric in the retelling. The irony is that it has to kill—or allow its soldiers to die— to receive them. Truth at the price of death of its young, the ultimate cannibalization, worse than any Greek myth of sacrifice.

"[. . .] the voice loud and small at the same time, insistent, calling "*Who? Who?* Who's in the next room?"

And to whom will the stories be told? And what will they matter?

And what happens to a nation unable to be an audience for its own life-and-death stories?

Herr does not present himself as an author as such: the Romantic "genius" who demands recognition for the unique, rare, one-of-a-kind text that he summoned in being; rather, *Dispatches* returns us to an earlier model of narration, not the novelist exactly (though the narrative is in part novelized), but the storyteller who draws on, and frames, a community's hoard of stories. He writes as the transcriber/interpreter of the stories that the living and the dead speak. There is no need to invent the story; the stories he conveys are already fantastic, grotesque, unbelievably believable precisely because they are obviously part of a national tradition which is, and has been, committed to doing the fantastic, the impossible—even when those acts require a blood sacrifice. *Dispatches* speaks of national nightmare by retelling the stories of those who made it happen. It is not his story alone; it is *our* story, a monstrous text we have collectively authored.

All the same, *Dispatches* is a unique, one-of-a-kind, rare book, one that only a genius could have written.

"Once we fanned over a little ville that had just been airstruck and the words of a song by Wingy Manone that I'd heard when I was a few years old snapped into my head, "Stop the War, these Cats is Killing

Themselves." Then we dropped, hovered, settled down into purple lz smoke, dozens of children broke from their hooches to run in toward the focus of our landing, the pilot laughing and saying, "Vietnam, man. Bomb 'em and feed 'em, bomb 'em and feed 'em."

Dispatches is suspicious of the written word, suspicious of the ways in which writing becomes an instrument of power, suspicious of the ways in which power contaminates and corrupts texts from the inside out by marshalling them on behalf of unworthy ends; at the same time, *Dispatches* is a text that honors the spoken word above the written word. The spoken word is invested with spontaneity, candor, unguarded soulfulness—in short Truth. This helps to explain why *Dispatches* constantly cleaves to spoken language, why it constantly quotes the colloquial, often crude language of the soldiers, their one-liner, cynical, in-the-know asides, their numbed revelations, their hyped-up conversations, their desperate monologues; also why it constantly quotes rock n' roll lyrics, which are seen as another variety of spoken language. *There* the book says is truth, as opposed to the lies and distortions of written language (official reports, articles, etc). *Dispatches* constantly struggles to transform itself into spoken language in order to distance itself from the degraded language of power. Only by approximating spoken language, only by distancing itself from the counterfeit currency of written discourse, can it hope to authenticate *the truths that are spoken in it.*

Is it a cliché to say that war breeds a pornography of spectatorship as well as a pornography of lifeless flesh? That it invites spectators to gaze upon the spectacle of dead bodies conjoined by an extremity of force? Bodies undone by an extremity of force? What is present in pornography is the physical force (e.g. the illusion of pleasure) that brings bodies together, contorts them into positions of pleasure or pain or both; what is absent (or present as a *trace*) are the social forces—in the case of visual pornography, capitalism; in the case of the Vietnamese War, anti-Communism, anti-nationalism, neo-colonialism—that have generated the *scene* of pornography—its stage, its actors, its characteristic offering to the audience of the performance as a spectacle to relish or to be repelled by. "Even when the picture was sharp and cleanly defined, something wasn't clear at all, something repressed that monitored the images and withheld their essential information. It may have legitimized my fascination, letting me look for as long as I wanted; I didn't have a language for it then but I remember now the shame I felt, like looking at first porn, all the porn in the world. I could have looked until my lamps went out and I still wouldn't have accepted the connection between a detached leg and the rest of a body, or the poses and positions that always happened (one day I'd hear it called "response-to-impact"), bodies wrenched too fast and violently into unbelievable contortion. Or the total impersonality of group death, making them lie anywhere and any way it left them, hanging over barbed wire or thrown promiscuously on top of other dead, or up into the trees like terminal acrobats, *Look what I can do.*"

In war, there are no clichés. Yet every war is a cliché.

"Talk about impersonating an identity, about locking into a role, about irony: I went to cover the war and the war covered me; an old story, unless of course you've never heard it. I went there behind the serious but crude belief that you had to be able to look at anything, serious because I acted on it and went, crude because I didn't know, it took the war to teach it, that you were as responsible for everything you saw as you were for everything you did. The problem was that you didn't always know what you were seeing until later, maybe years later, that a lot of it never made it in at all, it just stayed stored in your eyes. Time and information, rock and roll, life itself, the information isn't frozen, you are." Looking as a mode of seeing, seeing as a mode of recognizing, recognition as a mode of horror for "*you were as responsible for everything you saw as you were for everything you did.*" Against the horror of war, *Dispatches* asserts a poetics of relationship, a radical ethics, in which the subject/object world fades out like a scene in an old black and white film, like an old, used-up myth. A radical vision of love. To use another metaphor: subject/object duality is seen as a veil which causes us to misinterpret experience: seeing is not some detached activity that some mobile autonomous observer brings to something separate and fixed, something seen which is then left behind. Seeing itself is an act of responsibility inasmuch as that which is observed touches the observer; the observer takes *in* what is seen, *makes* it, and makes it a part of himself. He can no more leave it behind than he can leave behind his leg; it has become him. In seeing, you become responsible for what's seen because you use it for your own ends, and in using it, you owe it a part of your being. Nothing therefore is separate. The Vietnamese war: the vengeance of the "autonomous" ego upon a world it does not recognize as a world of its own, as itself, the world it made . . .

Silence: the weight of history.

Silence: the emptiness of history.

Silence: the writing of history.

Dispatches surges forward on a current of amped-up language, a war-fevered language on overdrive, language possessed by a sense of its own power—and powerlessness—but it also pays tribute to the *power* of silence. What is this power? The power to embarrass, the power to communicate *something* of the incommunicable, the power to respect that which cannot be signified by refusing to diminish it in words *that will not hold up*. Silence as the final guarantor of integrity, an essential gesture in acknowledging the force of power.

For all of *Dispatches'* stylistic brio, its linguistic virtuosity exists only as a stage for another kind of action. The text's performance climaxes on silence. *Dispatches* aspires to a state of pure silence.

Silence: the only way of honoring the dead. Also, the impossibility of honoring the dead in this way.

Apropos of silence, shame. Herr speaks of "American shame." For him, the most shameful people in the war were the war bureaucrats, much more shameful than the soldiers who actually did the killing: "It seemed the least of the war's contradictions that to lose your worst sense of American shame you had to leave the Dial Soapers in Saigon and a hundred headquarters who spoke good works and killed nobody themselves, and go out to the grungy men in the jungle who talked bloody murder and killed people all the time." Herr speaks of "losing your worst sense of American shame"; losing it entirely is not possible. It becomes something ineluctable, a part of one's identity, a "secret sharer."

What is shame? It is the intense recognition of failure or wrong doing which brings about a gnawing sense of isolation from others, or a fear of isolation from the embrace of the community. Shame is not an inert burden, but a corrosive, destructive, internal force that is transfiguring. Hence its sheer productive power: in dividing an individual or a nation from its cherished self-image, it requires the construction of painful new recognitions, chastened new identities—or else a tremendous expenditure of psychic energy as the individual or nation vainly tries to insulate itself from the monstrous truth about itself. The burden of maintaining an untrue identity, of constantly fighting a rearguard action against the *truth that shame speaks* requires the deliberate, ongoing, never-ending fictionalization of an identity, an act which, by necessity, can never be entirely successful. In a nation, the same thing, except that in the context of modern war, there arises the necessity of an entire class of "public relations" officers—Dial Soapers—who have the job of strangling shame in its crib. A war fought without shame will be unspeakably brutal and brutalizing because those who perform shameful acts will feel the need to punish those who "caused" them to deal with the psychic burden of shame. A shameful nation will perpetrate more and more terrible acts of aggression in order to prove to itself that it is not shameful, that it is not burdened by stigma, by an indefensible immorality. A shameful nation will always see itself as essentially *virtuous*, indeed as exceptionally virtuous.

Maps, mapping, ground: "In Saigon, it never mattered what they told you, even less when they actually seemed to believe it. Maps, charts, figures, projections, fly fantasies, names of places, of operations, commanders, of weapons; memories, guesses, second guesses, experiences (new, old, real, imagined, stolen); histories, attitudes—you could let it go, let it all go. If you wanted some war news in Saigon you had to hear it in stories brought from the field by friends, see it in the lost watchful eyes of the Saigonese, or do it like Trashman, reading the cracks in the sidewalks." Tainted by wish-fulfillment fantasies, all these maps show are the feverish, half-mad dreams of another century's would-be *conquistadores*. This much is evident. What is less so is that the ground itself is not self-evident, *there*: it too requires reading, interpretation. We have to become more like the Trashman, attentive to the cracks, and fissures of the ground, attentive to its shifts in meaning, its subtle semantic and political shadings, its unexpected widenings, its gaps, its sudden, swift, unexpected extensions. Is violence not rooted in the obstinate, perverse demand that the ground not move, that it correspond to our first or most cherished understanding of it, that it not change under our feet? Is violence not an expression of the doomed attempt to force the world to conform to an alien or antiquated arrangement? Are not maps representations of our desire to fix the ground, to arrest its flux, to give it a permanence that is always necessarily fictitious?

Wanton violence in war is always rooted in immaturity or insanity—or both. "There was such a dense concentration of American energy there, American and essentially adolescent, if that energy could have been channeled into anything more than noise, waste and pain, it would have lighted up Indochina for a thousand years." Perhaps it is the adolescent's capacity not merely for violence, but for insanity, that makes him the most desirable of warriors.

[. . .]"Nobody dies," as someone said in another war movie. This is the fantasy that the U.S. has sought to sell its people while mobilizing for war. The transparency of the lie poses no threat to its efficacy, for it provides the necessary fig-leaf for the repression of the truth. And if death arrives, it must arrive in the guise of nobility or heroism—idealizations that transfigure it, that deny it its sting, until it is no longer loss, but some recovered wholeness that reminds us of a virtue that has all but passed from this world. The fantasy of the Vietnamese War, as purveyed by the military, was of a casualty-free war, a fiction finally ruptured by a situation that refused to conform to the script. Ever since, the fantasy has become more, not less imperative; the lesson of Vietnam is not that people die in war, but that we cannot allow them to die in war; which is another way of saying that death cannot be seen. Death in war has passed from being an inevitability, a bloody emblem of the sacrifice made on behalf of some larger cause—indeed, proof of the value of that cause—to being top-secret, inadmissible, taboo.

And if nobody dies, we can never learn the value of a life, of life, of living—a curse that no civilization worth the name can bear for long.

If death is stricken from the record of war, every war hereafter will have to be a comedy.

Vietnam: bad theater as only America can do. Every war hereafter will need to be tightly-scripted, entertaining, good theater. And we are making progress . . .

Is all language prayer? Can things ever be signified by words? If language is a prayer, our words beseech one another, longing for a comprehension just out of reach. And yet mysteriously, sometimes, it happens: a connection is made. "After enough time passed and memory receded and settled, the name itself became a prayer, coded like all prayers to go past the extremes of petition and gratitude: Vietnam, Vietnam, Vietnam, say again, until the word lost all its old loads of pain, pleasure, horror, guilt, nostalgia." In this sense, *Dispatches* is also a prayer, a prayer for language to be adequate to the world, and to the meanings available in it, however desolate. Like a lover, the author addresses the world with an urgency borne out of the fierce need to make it feel what he has felt, to know what he knows, however imperfectly, however fleetingly . . .

"The Soldier's Prayer came in two versions: Standard, printed on a plastic-coated card by the Defense Department, and Standard Revised, impossible to convey because it got translated outside of language, into chaos, screams, begging, promises, threats, sobs, repetitions of holy names until their throats were cracked and dry, until some men had bitten through their collar points and rifle straps and even their dog-tag chains."

In war, all sound tends toward the inarticulate, towards silence. It is sovereign. It is precisely this sovereignty that *Dispatches* acknowledges, pays obeisance to—and disrupts. Language as regicide.

Yet it does so by telling a story, by writing about the stories heard, by reflecting upon what it means to signify the world in and through them. "Everywhere you went people said, "Well I hope you get a story," and everywhere you went you did." Everything is a story, everything has a story—which is why for Herr the official dispatches about the war cannot be the Story, why there are only *stories* (Nietzsche: "there is only perspective seeing") which can begin to do justice to the heterogeneity of experience. While the US Americanized Vietnam (less than many would have liked, but still), Vietnam Vietnamized American culture (less than many would have liked, but still), not least in the extent to which it assisted in the death of the Story, the realization that the one true, factual incontestable truth-version of things is a fiction. The death of the Story, Authority, Truth has been demonized in the postwar era as leading to fragmentation, relativism, immorality, chaos—"the center cannot hold"—but the Vietnam War stands as a monument to the dangers of the center—as well as the dangers of the center holding for too long. The question is not whether "the center" holds or not—but what kind of center is holding.

Or better yet: let us abolish the center and the presumptions of centrality. Let us concede to the inevitability of naming. But let us not idolize any single act of naming: let us, like Blake's innocent, write upon the water (only then is innocence possible). Let be be finale of seem.

"TIME IS ON MY SIDE, already written there across the first helmet I wore there. And underneath it, in smaller lettering that read more like a whispered prayer than an assertion, *No Lie, GI.*"

The effort of *Dispatches* is to let stories, fiction, do the work that the Truth cannot. *As if . . .*

Only in fiction is there truth. But it has to be *imagined*—and re-imagined.

Knowledge always exacts a price. What can you know—and at what cost? What happens to the self in war, or, in *warlike* circumstances? *Dispatches* circles back upon these questions time and again, the novel/memoir itself is organized formally around this circling, not a linear narrative with a triumphant ending, conclusive and final, but a shape of circling, of returning again and again to questions, rather than to an ultimate ground. In war, the question becomes especially urgent, precisely because the knowledge—knowledge of oneself and the world one is making—is acquired at such a price. "Overload was such a real danger, not as obvious as shrapnel or blunt like a 2,000 foot drop, maybe it couldn't kill you or smash you, but it could bend your aerial for you and land you on your hip. Levels of information were levels of dread, once it's out it won't go back in, you can't just blink it away or run the film backward out of consciousness. How many of those levels did you really want to hump yourself through, which plateau would you reach before you shorted out and started sending the messages back unopened." Worse than death is the death-in-life that these "levels of information," "levels of dread" created: hollow men; men hollowed out by violence, by seeing too much violence, by the knowledge of one's responsibility *for* it simply by being a witness *to* it. Ultimately, narratives, stories, created this violence of undoing—and the Faustian knowledge that flows from it.

Only other—new—narratives can remake that legacy, prevent another bad repetition of history, a fateful return to the old failures. This is the buried hope of *Dispatches*. It is, too, the buried imperative in Benjamin's catastrophic vision of history—which is at the same time a vision of redemption struggling to come into being: "A Klee painting named "Angelus Novus" shows an angel looking as though he is about to move away from something he is fixedly contemplating. His eyes are staring, his mouth is open, his wings are spread. This is how one pictures the angel of history. His face is turned toward the past. Where we peceive a chain of events, he sees one single catastrophe which keeps piling wreckage upon wreckage and hurls it in front of his feet. The angel would like to stay, awaken the dead, and make whole what has been smashed. But a storm is blowing from Paradise; it has got caught in his wings with such violence that the angel can no longer close them. This storm irresistibly propels him into the future to which his back is turned, while the pile of debris before him grows skyward. This storm is what we call progress" ("Theses on the Philosophy of History").

To rename oneself, to acquire a new identity, or to hold onto an older, imperiled one: this is the function of the writing on the body in war that Herr records: "On their helmets and flak jackets, they'd written the names of old operations, of girlfriends, their war names (FAR FROM FEARLESS, MICKEY'S MONKEY, AVENGER V, SHORT TIME SAFETY MOE), their fantasies (BORN TO LOSE, BORN TO RAISE

HELL, BORN TO KILL, BORN TO DIE), their ongoing information (HELL SUCKS, TIME IS ON MY SIDE, JUST YOU AND ME GOD—RIGHT?). This writing signifies the experiential uncertainty of war; it advertises a fear of war, nowhere more obviously than in the slogans with the most bravado. Writing here exists as a response to the blood-and-guts, life-and-death threat of war—this as opposed to the bland, white-washed, denatured writing of the military bureaucrats. The grunt's scrawled writing attempts to give voice to inarticulate pain, the silence of fear, the fear of losing one's identity; in short, this writing aspires to give the voicelessness of those fighting the war a voice; by contrast, the white papers of the bureaucrats would abolish it.

"And the grunts themselves knew: the madness, the bitterness, the horror, the doom of it. They were hip to it, and more: they savored it. It was no more insane than most of what was going down, and often enough, it had its refracted logic. "Eat the apple, fuck the Corps," they'd say, and write it on their helmets and flak jackets for their officers to see. (One kid had it tattooed on his shoulder.) And sometimes they'd look at you and laugh silently and long, the laugh on them and on you for being with them when you didn't have to be. And what could be funnier, really, given all that an eighteen-year-old boy could learn in a month of patrolling the Z? It was that joke at the deepest part of the blackest kernel of fear, and you could die laughing. They even wrote a song, a letter to the mother of a dead Marine, that went something like, "Tough shit, tough shit, your kid got greased, but what the fuck, he was just a grunt . . ." They got savaged a lot and softened a lot, their secret brutalized them and darkened them and very often it made them beautiful. It took no age, seasoning or education to make them know exactly where true violence resided" (103). This is what D.H. Lawrence saw at the beginning of the twentieth century: "But you have there the myth of the essential white America. All the other stuff, the love, the democracy, the floundering into lust, is a sort of by-play. The essential American soul is hard, isolate, stoic, and a killer. It has never yet melted" (*Studies in Classic American Literature*).

Yet the writing on the helmets and the flak jacket—like the mirthless laughter and the brutally ironic song—is not an expression of stoicism. It is an expression of protest that is protesting the systematic brutalization inflicted by war—and by the military which wages it. Writing then as protest, as an assertion of individuality—as well as the loss of it. However formulaic it may be, each grunt's graffiti aspires to the condition of writing in its fullest extension, each grunt to the condition of writer. Writing is to crystallize a mode of being, and an objection to the function their being is made to serve within the machinery of the military: this writing exceeds the system of military discipline, defies it, symbolically rejects it; but the military allows it as a necessary psychological safety valve. No accident that the graffiti is emblazoned across the head and the heart, the traditional sites for thinking and feeling, as if the sheer physical proximity of signs to organs demonstrates that these slogans are the most intimate expression of their being (the tattoo is merely the most radical expression of this logic). But also, the writing upon the body expresses not so much a talismanic belief in the power of writing to ward off death (although there might be traces of this wish there too), but, in locating the writing over the most vulnerable organs of the body, the brain and the heart, the grunt fatalistically acknowledges his own vulnerability to death, and preemptively curses the military for rendering him vulnerable to it, to dying, to physical agony, as well as to mental agony, whether as victim—or killer.

The essential American soul may be hard, isolate, and a killer—but, unexpectedly, it is also the soul of a dissident, who indicts killing—even as it becomes attracted to it. The American soul is neither one nor the other entirely, but torn, fatally divided by conflicting imperatives (idealism vs. duty, independence vs. authority), as well as by conflicting physical needs (safety vs. the thrill of adventure). Only this split, this self-division, this deep-seated ambivalence, can make sense of the geography of American history, in which there are vast, desert-like stretches of ruin, which give way, unexpectedly, to oases of splendor, shimmering like mirages on the edge of the horizon . . .

The other way to put it: The American soul is Lawrentian through and through . . .

Death as spectacle: one face of it is the face it assumes in the form of a spectacle, in which its sublime beauty momentarily outdistances its threat (or is it beautiful because of its threat)? Herr writes of war as not only as catastrophe and terror, but as an expression of beauty. The aesthetics of war, the aesthetics of death—this is the siren song of a civilization in which beauty is an émigré, and the price of admission is death, or the risk of it: "I remembered the way a Phantom pilot had talked about how beautiful the surface-to-air missiles looked as they drifted up toward his plane to kill him, and remembered myself how lovely .50-caliber tracers could be, coming at you as you flew at night in a helicopter, how slow and graceful, arching up easily, a dream, so remote from anything that could harm you. It could make you feel a total serenity, an elevation that put you above death, but that never lasted very long. One hit anywhere in the chopper would bring you back, bitten lips and white knuckles and all, and then you knew where you were. I was different with the incoming at Khe Sahn. You didn't get to watch the shells very often. You knew if you heard one, the first one, that you were safe, or at least saved. If you were still standing up and looking after that, you deserved anything that happened to you." Since Columbus, in the New World, beauty has been inflected and infected by danger: explorers, apprehending the natural sublimity of the landscape, always understood that they were making themselves vulnerable to death. American beauty: beauty conjoined with a death-defying heroism/folly. In the New World, "Death is the mother of beauty, mystical,/Within whose burning bosom we devise/Our earthly mothers waiting, sleeplessly" (Wallace Stevens, "Sunday Morning").

In this sense, *Dispatches* is a *beautiful* book: furious at the senselessness of the carnage, but finding in it too a terrible beauty, a distinctly American beauty . . .

The beauty of war: "At night you could lie out on some sandbags and watch the C-47's mounted with Vulcans doing their work. The C-47 was a standard prop flareship, but many of them carried a .20 and .762—mm guns on their doors, Mike-Mikes that could fire out 300 rounds per second, Gatling style, "a round in every square inch of a football field in less than a minute," as the handouts said. They used to call it Puff the Magic Dragon, but the Marines knew better: they named it Spooky. Every fifth round fired was a tracer, and when Spooky was working, everything stopped while the solid stream of violent red poured down out of the black sky. If you watched from a great distance, the stream would seem to dry up between bursts, vanishing slowly from air to ground like a comet tail, the sound of the guns disappearing too, a few seconds later. If you watched at close range, you couldn't believe that anyone could have the courage to deal with that, night after night, week after week, and you cultivated a respect for the Viet Cong and NVA who had crouched under it every night now for months. It was awesome, worse than anything the Lord had ever put down upon Egypt, and at night, you'd hear the Marines talking, watching it, yelling, "Get Some!" until they grew quiet and someone would say, "Spooky understands." The nights were very beautiful. Night was when you really had the least to fear and feared the most. You could go through some very bad numbers at night." War as spectacle, technological marvel, and death-mask: beauty-as-death, death-as-beauty, apotheosis and nadir, civilization's dead-end, all at once.

Reading this, it is difficult not to think of Walter Benjamin's warning against the seductions of fascism: "Marinetti says in his manifesto on the Ethiopian colonial war: "For twenty-seven years we Futurists have rebelled against the branding of war anti-aesthetic . . . Accordingly, we state: . . . War is beautiful because it establishes man's dominion over the subjugated machinery by means of gas masks, terrifying megaphones, flame throwers, and small tanks. War is beautiful because it enriches a flowering meadow with the fiery orchids of machine guns. War is beautiful because it combines the gunfire, the cannonades, the cease-fire, the scents, and the stench of putrefaction into a symphony. War is beautiful because it creates new architecture, like that of the big tanks, the geometrical formation flights, the smoke spirals from burning villages, and many others [. . .]" This formulation has the virtue of clarity [. . .] The destructiveness of war furnishes proof that society has not been mature enough to incorporate technology as its organ, that technology has not been sufficiently developed to cope with the elemental forces of society [. . .] Imperialistic war is a rebellion of technology which collects, in the form of "human material," the claims to which society has denied its natural material. Instead of draining rivers, society directs a human stream into human trenches; instead of dropping seeds from airplanes, it drops incendiary bombs over cities [. . .] This is evidently the consummation of "*l'art pour l'art*." Mankind, which in Homer's time was an object of contemplation for the Olympian gods, now is one for itself. Its self-alienation has reached such a degree that it can experience its own self-destruction as an aesthetic pleasure of the first order."

America: the land of the future, the land of the Futurists.

Dispatches desires to speak for those who about to die, those who are so close to death that they are almost ghosts, specters in the making. It feels a burden of responsibility to them, to their experience, to the thin red line that they walk, even as they perform atrocities, unspeakable acts, as well as heroic ones on behalf of morally bankrupt principles. (The ungovernable eccentricity of love). Herr sees war as a system that brutalizes and corrupts, and not merely its victims, but its perpetrators. This brutalization, this coarsening, renders them the living dead: *Dispatches* longs to give voice to the pain of this self-alienation, this self-destruction, this spectricality; it offers America the uncomfortable position of being responsible for the devastation Herr witnesses. We become, that is, voyeurs of the maniacally-inventive, technologically-driven forms of destruction unleashed in Vietnam.

In positioning us as voyeurs, *Dispatches* suggests the *pornography* of the war, (its violation and abject meaninglessness): "There were choices everywhere, but they were never choices you could hope to make. There was even some small chance for personal style in your recognition of the one thing you feared more than any other. You could die in a sudden bloodburning crunch as your chopper hit the ground like dead weight, you could fly apart so that your pieces would never be gathered, you could take one neat round in the lung and go out hearing only the bubble of the last few breaths, you could die in the last stage of malaria with that faint tapping in your ears and that could happen to you after months of firefights and rockets and machine guns. Enough, too many, were saved for that and you always hoped that no irony would attend your passing. You could end in a pit somewhere with a spike through you, everything stopped forever except for the one or two motions, purely involuntary, as though you could kick it all away and come back. You could fall down dead so that the medics would have to spend half an hour for the hole that killed you, getting more and more spooked as the search went on. You could be shot, mined, grenaded, rocketed, mortared, blown up and away so that your leavings had to be dropped into a sagging poncho and carried to Graves Registration, that's all she wrote. It was almost marvelous."

Dispatches wants at the same time to be faithful to the idea of justice, which is nothing more than a ghost, a haunting, which reminds the community of what it is *not*. To make that which *is* ghostly, a haunting: this is the desire of writing . . .

Wandering and home: the fate and desire of ghosts: the fate of ghosts is to wander, but to search for home; the same true of writing.

Souvenirs: fragments from the past, reminders of who were are, where we've come from. Moreover, souvenirs are fragments symbolic of the past (they can only be *symbols* of the past, never the past itself). War souvenirs, no less, are tokens of identity, reminders of the refashioning of the self that has taken place in and through violence. Like writing, they are commemorative, markers of the development of the self in time; but they are also tokens of the violence of war (the *boundarylessness* of it). As trophies of victory, they testify to a rebirth through violence. Signs of what their violence has done, war souvenirs are also the soldiers' signs of what has been undone: their former selves, their old world. Perhaps this is why they become fetishized objects: having lost their old selves, their old world, veterans need to remind themselves of their new selves, their new world—something being better than nothing. That so many of these tokens display graphic forms of separation (cutting, severing, dismembering) suggests the unmaking of the world that their violence has brought about. War souvenirs: autobiographies of lost souls: "[. . .] a Marine came up to Lengle and me and asked if we'd like to take a look at some pictures he'd taken [. . .] There were hundreds of these albums in Vietnam, thousands, and they all seemed to contain the same pictures: the obligatory Zippo-lighter shot ("All right, let's burn these hootches and move out"); the severed head shot, the head often resting on the chest of the dead man or being held up by a smiling Marine, or a lot of heads, arranged in a row, with a burning cigarette in each of the mouths, the eyes open ("Like they're looking at you man, it's scary'); the VC suspect being dragged over the dust by a half-track or being hung by his heels in some jungle clearing; the very young dead with AK-47s in their hands ("How old would you say that kid was?" the grunts would ask. "Twelve, thirteen? You just can't tell with gooks"); a picture of a Marine holding an ear or maybe two ears or, as in the case of a guy I knew near Pleiku, a whole necklace made of ears, "love beads" as its owner called them."

Gooks: inhumans, language ghosts. Reincarnation through renaming: a "gook" is infinitely easier to kill than a flesh-and-blood human being whose face mirrors your own. Language as a means of war: a word that licenses violence. (Kurtz: "Exterminate all the brutes!"). And a balm to the conscience. Ghostly etymology of "gooks": racial epithet applied to Haitians by American troops stationed there between 1915 and 1934 as part of a military occupation to prevent uprisings. A "gook" literally signifies "a foreigner." So the term has a history of being used by Americans in foreign places, where *they* are the foreigners, to naturalize the American presence and de-legitimize the presence of the natives: "gooks" transforms them into something illegitimate, something "foreign," undesirable, if not unacceptable. Ghosts in their own land. With an Alice-in-Wonderland power, it transforms occupier into native, and native into foreigner. (In the word "gooks" is inscribed the colonial mentality, indeed the colonial history of the US in the twentieth-century). Racially inflected, it is a term of great plasticity; like a virus, it can lie dormant for decades and then suddenly spring into life with renewed vigor as it draws life from a new host population. Dormant now (a ghost), it awaits its next incarnation . . .

Vietnam: America's ghost; America: Vietnam's ghost. Each haunting the other, making of the other a powerful, spectral no-man's land of memory and hurt, memory's badlands that know no border with the here-and-now.

(Other ghosts: I too am wandering through Herr's text, returning to its no-man's-land again and again, willing it into being, never wanting it to go away, but doomed to become spectral, one day to pass away, just like all the others. I am thinking now—and have been all the while—of my cousin, A.M, who, like many others, died in Vietnam, looking for an identity, looking for a better self, as his last letters home, his carefully-composed, handwritten letters, show. Killed in action with no chance of atonement. Did he know they were dead letters? He must have. Ghost letters, which these letters, these black marks on a white page cannot redeem . . .)

Works Cited

Primary Texts

Bradford, William. *Of Plymouth Plantation 1620–1647*. Samuel Eliot Morison, editor. New York: Knopf, 2001.

Dickinson, Emily. *The Complete Poems of Emily Dickinson*. Thomas H. Johnson, editor Boston: Little, Brown and Company, 1960.

Dickinson, Emily *The Letters of Emily Dickinson*. Thomas H. Johnson, editor. Cambridge, Massachusetts: Harvard University Press, 1996.

Herr, Michael. *Dispatches*. New York: Vintage, 1991.

Melville, Herman. 'Bartleby, the Scrivener' in *Billy Budd and Other Stories*, edited and introduced by Frederick Busch. New York: Penguin Classics, 1986.

Other Texts Cited

Benjamin, Walter. 'Theses on the Philosophy of History.' *Illuminations*. New York: Schocken Books, 1969.

Berger, John. 'The Hour of Poetry.' *The Sense of Sight*. New York: Vintage, 1985.

Blake, William. *The Marriage of Heaven and Hell. Jerusalem: Selected Poems and Prose.* Hazard Adams, editor. New York: Holt, Rinehart and Winston, 1970.

Blanchot, Maurice. Ann Smock, translator. *Writing of the Disaster*. Lincoln: University of Nebraska Press, 1995.

Conrad, Joseph. *Heart of Darkness*. New York: Oxford University Press, 2003.

Derrida, Jacques. 'Text Read at Louis Althusser's Funeral.' *deconstruction: a reader*. Martin McQuillan, editor. New York: Routledge, 2001.

Eliot, T.S. 'Gerontion.' *Collected Poems, 1909–1962*. New York: Harcourt, Brace and World, 1963.

Eliot, T.S. 'The Waste Land.' *Collected Poems, 1909–1962*. New York: Harcourt, Brace and World, 1963.

Faulkner, William. *As I Lay Dying*. New York: Vintage, 1991.

Geisst, Charles R. *Wall Street: A History*. New York: Oxford University Press, 1997.

Graham, Jorie. 'Emergency.' *The Errancy*. Hopewell, New Jersey: The Ecco Press, 1997.

Howe, Susan. *My Emily Dickinson*. Berkeley: North Atlantic Books, 1985.

Jabès, Edmond. *A Foreigner Carrying in the Crook of His Arm a Tiny Book*. Rosmarie Waldrop, translator. Hanover and London: Wesleyan University Press, 1993.

Jabès, Edmond. 'The Moment After.' *deconstruction: a reader*. Martin McQuillan, editor. New York: Routledge, 2001. pp.80–87.

Jameson, Fredric. *The Political Unconsciousness: Narrative as a Socially Symbolic Act*. Ithaca, New York: Cornell University Press, 1981.

Lawrence, D.H. *Studies in Classic American Literature*. New York: The Viking Press, 1970.

Lukács, Georg. *The Theory of the Novel*. Cambridge, Massachusetts: MIT Press, 1985.

Malick, Terrence. *The Thin Red Line*. Twentieth Century Fox, 1998. Based on James Jones' *The Thin Red Line*. New York: Delta, 1998.

Lawrence, D.H. *Studies in Classic American Literature*. New York: The Viking Press, 1970.

Marx, Karl. *The Eighteenth Brumaire of Louis Bonaparte*. New York: International Publishers Co., 1963.

Nietzsche, Friedrich. *Beyond Good and Evil*. *The Basic Writings of Nietzsche*. Walter Kaufmann, editor and translator. New York: The Modern Library. 1968. pp.179–360.

O'Brien, Tim. 'How to Tell a True War Story.' *The Things They Carried*. New York: Broadway, 1998.

Oppen, George. 'Of Being Numerous.' *The Collected Poems of George Oppen*. New York: New Directions, 1975.

Palmer, Michael. *At Passages*. New York: New Directions, 1995

Pound, Ezra. 'Hugh Selwyn Mauberley.' *Poems and Translations*. Richard Sieburth, editor. New York: Library of America, 2003.

Rowlandson, Mary. *A True History of the Captivity and Restoration of Mrs. Mary Rowlandson*. *American Captivity Narratives*. Gordon M. Sayre, editor. Boston: Houghton Mifflin, 2000.

Rushdie, Salman. *Imaginary Homelands*. New York: Penguin, 1992.

Scarry, Elaine. *The Body in Pain: The Making and Unmaking of the World*. New York: Oxford University Press, 1985.

Shakespeare, William. *The Tempest*. John Hollander, editor. New York: Penguin, 1999.

Stevens, Wallace. *The Collected Poems of Wallace Stevens*. New York: Knopf, 2000.

Williams, William Carlos. *Spring and All. Imaginations*. Walter Schott, editor. New York: New Directions, 1970.

Winthrop, John. "A Model of Christian Charity." *The American Puritans*. Perry Miller, editor. New York: Columbia University Press, 1982.

Yeats, William Butler. *The Collected Poems of W.B. Yeats*. Richard Finneran, editor. New York: Scribner, 1996.

www.ingramcontent.com/pod-product-compliance
Lightning Source LLC
Chambersburg PA
CBHW030337020726
47493CB00004B/1305